Ginn English

Richard L. Venezky
Carol J. Fisher

Ginn and Company

Acknowledgments: Grateful acknowledgment is made to the following publishers, authors, and agents for permission to use and adapt copyrighted materials:

Atheneum Publishers, Inc., for "We Could Be Friends" by Myra Cohn Livingston, in *The Way Things Are and Other Poems.* Copyright © 1974 by Myra Cohn Livingston. A Margaret K. McElderry Book. Reprinted with the permission of Atheneum Publishers.

Delacorte Press for the poem "Dictionary" excerpted from the book *Laughing Time* by William Jay Smith. Copyright © 1953, 1955, 1956, 1957, 1959, 1968, 1974, 1977, 1980 by William Jay Smith. Reprinted by permission of Delacorte Press/Seymour Lawrence.

E. P. Dutton, Inc., for the poem "Halfway Down" from *When We Were Very Young* by A. A. Milne. Copyright © 1924 by E. P. Dutton & Co., Inc. and renewed, 1952 by A. A. Milne. Reprinted by permission of the publishers, E. P. Dutton, Inc.

Harcourt Brace Jovanovich, Inc., for "Paper I" by Carl Sandburg. From *The Complete Poems of Carl Sandburg,* copyright 1950 by Carl Sandburg; renewed 1978 by Margaret Sandburg, Helga Sandburg Crile and Janet Sandburg. Reprinted by permission of Harcourt Brace Jovanovich, Inc.

Harper & Row, Publishers, Inc., for "Bedtime" from *Poems for Children* by Eleanor Farjeon (text only). (J. B. Lippincott) Copyright 1933, 1961 by Eleanor Farjeon. Reprinted by permission of Harper & Row, Publishers, Inc.

Little, Brown and Company for the poem "Eletelephony" from *Tirra Lirra* by Laura E. Richards. Copyright 1932 by Laura E. Richards; © renewed 1960 by Hamilton Richards. By permission of Little, Brown and Company. Also for the poem beginning "A bird came down the walk:" (first verse only) from *Poems for Youth* by Emily Dickinson, edited by Alfred Leete Hampson. Copyright, 1918, 1919, 1924, 1929, 1932, 1934 by Martha Dickinson Bianchi.

McClelland and Stewart Limited for the poem "Halfway Down" by A. A. Milne. From *When We Were Very Young* by A. A. Milne reprinted by permission of The Canadian Publishers, McClelland and Stewart Limited, Toronto.

William Morrow & Company, Inc., for the sentences about the Cardiff Giant in Section C on page 88 and the sentences about Lillian Leitzel in Section D on page 89. Based on pages 1243–44 and 786–88, respectively, in *The People's Almanac #2* by David Wallechinsky and Irving Wallace. Copyright © 1978 by David Wallechinsky and Irving Wallace. By permission of William Morrow & Company.

G. P. Putnam's Sons for the poem "The Picnic" by Dorothy Aldis. Reprinted by permission of G. P. Putnam's Sons from *Hop, Skip & Jump* by Dorothy Aldis. Copyright 1934; renewed © 1961 by Dorothy Aldis.

The dictionary entries and guide words on page 152 are abridged from *Scott, Foresman Beginning Dictionary* by E. L. Thorndike and Clarence L. Barnhart. Copyright © 1979, Scott, Foresman and Company.

Photographs: Peter Arnold, Inc./Steve J. Krassemann, 57; Philip Jon Bailey, 275; Bettmann Archive, Inc., 191, 198; Lee Boltin, 189; Leo de Wys, Inc./Barbara Wolf, 291; Farrell Grehan, 193; Global Focus/Richard Al Miller, 29; NASA, 35; Michael Pateman, 65, 302; The Picture Cube/C. T. Seymour, 31; Siteman Studios, 8–9, 27, 42, 55, 87, 105, 109, 115, 128, 138–139, 159, 163, 171, 205, 211, 235, 247, 261, 272–273, 287, 293, 303; Taurus Photos/G. R. Richardson, 283.

Illustrators: Bob Barner   Maryann Cocca
Patrick Blackwell   John Killgrew
Bettina Borer   Susan Swan
David Cain

Contents

3

2 Giving and Taking Messages

3 Writing Letters

4

We Could Be Friends

We could be friends
Like friends are supposed to be.
You, picking up the telephone
Calling me

　　to come over and play
　　or take a walk,
　　finding a place
　　to sit and talk,

Or just goof around
Like friends do,
Me, picking up the telephone
Calling you.

　　　　　　　　　—*Myra Cohn Livingston*

1

Ordering
Information

SKILLS TO BUILD ON

Sentences and Punctuation
Subjects and Predicates
Alphabetical Order
Yes-No and WH-Questions

PRACTICAL APPLICATIONS

Learning about Paragraphs
Listening for Information

Sentences

> **A *sentence* tells a whole thought.**
> <u>Sentence:</u> I see the beach.
> <u>Not a sentence:</u> the beach

Sentences tell complete thoughts. Not every group of words is a sentence.

Look at this group of words.

Hawaii has a black beach.

The group of words tells a complete thought. It is a sentence.

Look at these groups of words.

castle of sand   traveled by boat

They are not complete thoughts. What do you know about the castle of sand? Who traveled? See how these words can be made into sentences.

I built a castle of sand. We traveled by boat.

A sentence begins with a capital letter. Each sentence above ends with a period (.).

Now look at the next groups of words.

The sea washed the castle away.
Hawaii has

Which is a sentence? Which is not a sentence?

Words in a sentence must be in a certain order.
A sentence must make sense. Look at these words.
Put the words in an order that makes sense.

Kate sand. in dug the
She likes beach. the

PRACTICE

A. (Oral) Three groups of words are sentences.
Three are not. Say the sentences.

1. Hawaii is our newest state.
2. eight big islands in
3. It is not in North America.
4. the middle of the ocean
5. It has volcanoes.
6. beaches and sand

B. (Written) Put the words in an order that
makes sense. The capital letters and
punctuation marks are clues.

Example: Sailors maps. special use
Sailors use special maps.

1. Maps pictures. are
2. Some roads. show
3. Others countries. show
4. A map streets. may show
5. Maps sizes. all are
6. Maps us. help

APPLY

Write two sentences. Write one about your
street. Write one about your town or city.

Kinds of Sentences

There are different kinds of sentences.

Statement: I read the book.

Question: Did you read it?   Exclamation: Look out!

Every sentence has a job to do. The jobs are not all the same. Some sentences tell something. These sentences are called *statements.* A statement ends with a period.

Look at this statement.

The Liberty Bell is an old bell.

Some sentences ask something. These sentences are called *questions.* A question ends with a question mark.

Look at these questions.

Who cracked the Liberty Bell?
Will we see it?

Some sentences show strong feelings. These sentences are called *exclamations.* They end with exclamation marks.

What feelings do these exclamations show?

We won the race!
Stop pushing me right now!

PRACTICE

A. (Oral) Read each sentence. Tell if the sentence is a *statement* or a *question*.

Example: My family drove to Kentucky.
statement

1. There is a famous cave in Kentucky.
2. Have you seen it?
3. Do animals live in it?
4. Some fish there have no eyes.
5. They live in Echo River.
6. Where is Echo River?

B. (Written) Read each sentence. Write *S* if the sentence is a statement. Write *Q* if it is a question. Write *E* if it is an exclamation.

Example: Do grapes have seeds?
Q

1. Are grapes hard to grow?
2. Don't step on the grapes!
3. Where did they find grapes?
4. California has many vineyards.
5. New York has a lot.
6. Do grapes grow in your state?

APPLY

Write three sentences about school. Write one statement. Write one question. Write one exclamation.

Beginning and Ending Sentences

> **A sentence begins with a capital letter. It ends with a punctuation mark.**
>
> <u>Statement:</u> This is a sentence.
> <u>Question:</u> Is this a sentence?
> <u>Exclamation:</u> What a great sentence this is!

A sentence has a beginning and an end. The beginning is a capital letter. The end is a punctuation mark.

Look at these sentences.

We saw a parade.   It was a big one.

These sentences are statements. Remember that a statement tells something. It ends with a period.

Look at these questions.

Was the parade exciting?   Did you like it?

A question asks something. It ends with a question mark.

An exclamation shows strong feeling. It ends with an exclamation mark. The next sentence is an exclamation.

A mouse was leading the parade!

PRACTICE

A. (Oral) Each sentence is missing something. It could be a capital letter. It could be a punctuation mark. Tell what is missing.

> **Example:** Walt Disney made many films
> **a period**

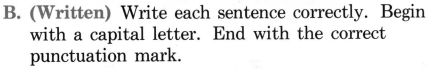

1. were they all cartoons?
2. Some were nature films
3. his first big star was a mouse.
4. I don't believe it
5. Haven't you heard of Mickey Mouse
6. his first film was in 1928.

B. (Written) Write each sentence correctly. Begin with a capital letter. End with the correct punctuation mark.

> **Example:** where is the yeast
> **Where is the yeast?**

1. yeast is used to make bread
2. is the yeast in this cup
3. the yeast is growing
4. it looks terrible
5. is it alive
6. it is alive
7. don't be silly
8. will we make bread

APPLY

Write two sentences about a game you like to play. Make one sentence an exclamation.

Correcting Sentences

Sentences should not run together.

Incorrect: It is raining it is windy outside.

Some sentences should be shortened.

Too Long: I will go outside and I will wear boots
and my feet will not get wet.

Sometimes you may forget a period. The next sentence may not start with a capital letter. The sentences run together. They do not make sense.

Look at the group of words below.

Hurricanes are big storms they used to have only women's names now they have men's names, too.

Where would you put capital letters? Where would you put punctuation marks?

Look at this long sentence.

In summer we watch shooting stars and August is the best month and we stay up to watch.

Do not join a lot of sentences with the word *and.*

Better: In summer we watch shooting stars. August is the best month. We stay up to watch.

PRACTICE

A. (Written) These sentences run on and on. Write better ones. Think how you fixed the sentences about hurricanes on page 16.

1. ~~Put an ice cube on a bug bite it will itch less baking soda works well, too.~~
2. Bees live and work together bees live in hives bees make honey.
3. Summer is vacation time it is hot and sunny summer is great for swimming and boating.

B. (Written) Write better sentences. Look at the bottom of page 16 for help.

4. Mars is near Earth and Jupiter is next to Mars and Jupiter has fourteen moons and Jupiter is much bigger than Mars.
5. Four of Jupiter's moons are very bright and some moons are not as bright and it took longer to discover them.
6. We are sending rockets into space and they are sending back pictures and maybe we can learn more about the planets.

APPLY

Think about going to another planet. Write two sentences about the trip.

Review the Basics I

A. Sentences

Three groups of words are sentences. Five are not. Write the sentences. *(pages 10–11)*

1. New York City lions
2. The library has two.
3. very famous lions
4. their pictures
5. the Fifth Avenue
6. The lions are statues.
7. cards showing pictures
8. New York City has a zoo.

Put the words in an order that makes sense. The capital letters and punctuation marks are clues. *(pages 10–11)*

9. A flying object Arizona. hit
10. This ago. happened long
11. It hole. big a made
12. The hole wide. mile is a
13. People it. love
14. They go it. to see
15. They pictures of the hole. take

B. Kinds of Sentences

Read each sentence. Write *S* if it is a statement. Write *Q* if it is a question. Write *E* if it is an exclamation. *(pages 12–13)*

1. Have you seen the Statue of Liberty?
2. It stands in New York Harbor.
3. The statue was sent here in pieces.

4. Do you know what it weighs?
5. It weighs more than 200 tons.
6. You should see it!
7. Forty people can stand in its head.
8. What a view they have!
9. How can you get there?

C. Beginning and Ending Sentences

Write each sentence correctly. Begin with a capital letter and end with the correct punctuation mark. *(pages 14–15)*

1. a boat club is in Newport, Rhode Island
2. it was named for a woman
3. what was her name
4. her name was Ida Lewis
5. she lived at the lighthouse
6. why was she special
7. she helped many people
8. she saved them from drowning

D. Correcting Sentences

These sentences run on and on. Write better ones. *(pages 16–17)*

1. New York City is big it has many animals I like the lions best.
2. Lions are in the zoo lions are in the jungle some lions are in New York City.

A Basic Sentence

Now you know many facts about sentences. Still, not every sentence you write will be perfect. You might be in a hurry and leave out a part. You might forget a capital letter or a punctuation mark.

Ask yourself if each sentence is a complete thought. Is something missing? Are the words in the right order? Do they make sense?

Look at these groups of words.

buildings shaped like milk bottles
One is in Spokane, Washington.
one is in Boston, Massachusetts

Two groups need to be fixed to make sentences. How would you fix them?

Check everything you write. Fix the mistakes you find. Use what you know to make your sentences better. Read the Reminders.

REMINDERS

1. A sentence tells a complete thought.
2. A sentence begins with a capital letter.
3. A sentence ends with a punctuation mark.
4. A statement ends with a period.
5. A question ends with a question mark.
6. An exclamation ends with an exclamation mark.

PRACTICE/APPLY

A. (Written) Some groups of words are sentences. Some are not. If the group is not a sentence, write *not a sentence.* Write *S* for a statement. Write *Q* for a question. Write *E* for any sentence that is an exclamation.

Examples: the open door   That's great!
         not a sentence   **E**

1. helping save energy
2. You can help save energy.
3. Do you close the door behind you?
4. Don't forget the lights!
5. should not drive faster than
6. You should be careful with water.
7. leaving water running
8. Do you wear warm sweaters?

B. (Written) Each sentence below has a mistake. Fix each sentence.

Example: you will love it!
        You will love it!

9. Apple sauce is good food it is easy to cook you should make some.
10. First peel the apples and take out the seeds
11. Then cut the apples into pieces
12. put the apples and some water in a pan.
13. Cover the pan
14. cook the sauce slowly.
15. Does it taste good

Alphabetical Order

How do you find one word in a long list? It is easy if the list is in alphabetical order. To alphabetize words, you put them in ABC order. Put words that start with *A* before words that start with *B.* Put words that start with *B* before words that begin with *C.*

Read these words.

> **a**nt **b**ee **c**at **d**og **h**orse **p**ig

The words are in ABC order.

Which group of names is not in ABC order? How would you fix it?

> **Bob** **Chris** **Dot**   **Ana** **Pat** **Kim**

What if some words start with the same letter? Then you must look at the second letter.

Look at these words.

> **f**a̲ce **f**i̲nger **f**o̲ot **f**r̲eckle

They all start with *f.* They are in alphabetical order by the second letter.

Check the next groups of words.

> Jan   Jean   Jimmy   John
> chipmunk   cow   cat   crab

Which is not in ABC order? How can you fix it?

PRACTICE

A. (Oral) Say each group of words in alphabetical order.

> **Example:** floor   wall   door
> **door   floor   wall**

1. duck   bunny   puppy
2. camel   deer   ant
3. fox   squirrel   elephant
4. fish   hamster   gerbil
5. bird   pig   duck
6. Joshua   Chris   Kim
7. Rachel   Jane   Carlos
8. pony   horse   cow

B. (Written) Write each group of words in alphabetical order.

> **Example:** Josie   Jim   Jessie
> **Jessie   Jim   Josie**

1. shark   snake   spider
2. plum   pear   apple
3. squash   potato   bean
4. truck   car   subway
5. cab   bus   bike
6. chair   desk   door
7. window   wall   ceiling
8. Mina   Melba   Manuel

APPLY

Look at the Example words in Practice A. Write two sentences about the words.

Parts of a Book

There are many kinds of books. You read textbooks, storybooks, and poetry books. You look at picture books. You can see that every book is different. Name some other kinds of books.

Books are alike in some ways, too. Books have covers that tell their names. The name of a book is called its *title*. The title helps you know what is inside the book. What is the name of this book?

Most books also have contents pages. A *table of contents* lists the parts of the book in order. It tells on what page each part begins.

Many books have an index at the back. The *index* lists the page numbers for all the subjects in the book. The subjects are shown in alphabetical order. Suppose you had a book titled *Math Facts*. The index would list *addition* near the beginning. It would list *subtraction* nearer the end.

PRACTICE

A. (Oral) Find the answers to these questions. Use the contents pages of this book.

> **Example:** How many units are in this book?
> **7 units**

1. On what page does Unit 1 start?
2. How many lessons are in the first unit?
3. What is the title of Unit 3?
4. On what page does Unit 3 start?
5. How many lessons are in Unit 3?
6. What unit has the most lessons?
7. On what page does the index start?
8. On what page does the Handbook start?
9. Which unit is called *Telling Stories*?

B. (Written) Find the answers to these questions. Write the page numbers. Use the index of this book.

> **Example:** Where would you find abbreviations?
> **66–67, 135, 322, 323, 334**

1. Where would you find messages?
2. Where would you find poetry?
3. Where would you find prefixes?
4. Where would you find the telephone directory?
5. Where would you find a riddle?

APPLY

Write two sentences about this English book.

Using a Telephone Book

The telephone book, or directory, lists phone numbers. Most numbers are listed by people's last names. The names are in alphabetical order.

To find names quickly, think of the book in three parts. Last names that begin with *A-F* will be in the first part. Last names that begin with *G-P* will be near the middle. Last names that begin with *Q-Z* will be near the end.

Look at the sample.

Gale—Hyland	
Gale Jean D Clare Av	555-4397
Gennert Steven Bond Rd	555-1661
Gibson E R 23 Main	555-3972
Gloff Clark 133 Crest	555-8321
Golden John 28 Great Rd	555-0173
Gray Susan 19 Davis Rd	555-7845
Gray Thomas 34 Elm Rd	555-0285
Gum's Paper Store 8 Oakview	555-0038
Hall Adele 183 High	555-7611
Hall Fred 183 High	555-1310
Hill Bob & Sue 284 West Av	555-5532
Homes Wm P 781 Beacon	555-6009

The *guide words* are the names at the top of each page. The first guide word tells the first name listed. The next guide word gives the last name on the page.

The guide words are *Gale* and *Hyland*. They tell you that names starting with *G* and *H* are on this page. Names that come before *Gale* in ABC order are on pages before this one. Names that come after *Hyland* are on pages after this one.

PRACTICE

A. (Oral) Answer the questions. Find the answers in the sample on page 26.

1. What are the guide words?
2. On what street does John Golden live?
3. What is John Golden's phone number?
4. What is the address of Adele Hall?
5. What is the address of Fred Hall?
6. Do they have the same phone number?
7. What is Clark Gloff's number?

B. (Written) Write answers to the questions. Use the sample.

1. What does Gum's sell?
2. What is Susan Gray's phone number?
3. Thomas Gray lives on Elm Road. What is his number?
4. Which person named Gray lives on Davis Road?
5. What is E. R. Gibson's number?

APPLY

Write two sentences. Tell when you might use the phone book.

Subjects

> **Every sentence has a subject. The *subject* tells whom or what the sentence is about.**
>
> "The wheat grew." What grew? The wheat did.

Every sentence has a subject. The *subject* tells whom or what the sentence is about.

Look at this sentence.

Texas|is a big state.

This sentence is about Texas. *Texas* is the subject of the sentence.

The subject of a sentence may be one word. It may be a group of words, too.

Look at this sentence.

Two presidents|were born there.

The sentence is about two presidents. The subject is *Two presidents.*

Look at these sentences.

Rice grows in Texas.
Our vacation began in Austin.

The subject is usually in the first part of a sentence. What is the subject in each?

PRACTICE

A. (Oral) Tell the subject of each sentence. The subject may be one or more than one word.

> **Example:** My family drove to Texas.
> **My family**

1. My sister was surprised at its size.
2. Many things surprised me.
3. Cotton grows in Texas.
4. Cattle are raised there, too.
5. The Houston Ship Canal has big ships.
6. Oil wells pump oil.
7. Many cattle are near Fort Worth.
8. Our car broke down.
9. The trip ended.

B. (Written) These sentences have no subjects. Make up a subject for each sentence. Write each subject.

> **Example:** _____ wear boots.
> **Some people**

1. _____ ran down the road.
2. _____ like to go to rodeos.
3. _____ live on ranches.
4. _____ rides a horse.
5. _____ is fed to animals.
6. _____ eat grass.

APPLY

Think about a famous person who might visit your town. Write two sentences about the visit. Draw a line under each subject.

Predicates

> **Every sentence has a predicate. The *predicate* tells what the subject does, is, or has.**
>
> "Kevin went to South Dakota." What did Kevin do? He went to South Dakota.

You know that the subject of a sentence tells whom or what the sentence is about. The *predicate* tells more about the subject. It tells what the subject does, is, or has.

Read this sentence.

> **Kevin|stands in the center of the United States.**

The subject of the sentence is *Kevin*. To find the predicate, ask what Kevin does or is. Kevin *stands in the center of the United States.* This group of words is the predicate.

Read the next sentence.

> **The place|is in South Dakota.**

What words tell more about the place? This group of words is the predicate.

A predicate can be a group of words or one word. What is the predicate in this sentence?

> **Kevin's family travels.**

PRACTICE

A. (Oral) Tell the predicate of each sentence.

> **Example:** Our family likes South Dakota.
> **likes South Dakota**

1. Several huge statues are there.
2. One statue is at Mount Rushmore.
3. Many people visit it.
4. The faces of presidents are carved from stone.
5. A bigger statue is being made.
6. It will be over 600 feet tall.
7. It is carved with a bulldozer.
8. It shows Chief Crazy Horse.
9. Thunderhead Mountain is the place.

B. (Written) These sentences have no predicates. Write a predicate to complete each sentence.

> **Example:** The bus _____ .
> **stopped at the light**

1. Some people _____ .
2. The train _____ .
3. The park _____ .
4. A big city _____ .
5. The street _____ .
6. The boys and girls _____ .
7. Our school _____ .
8. A car _____ .

APPLY

Think of a special place you have gone to see. Write two sentences about it. Draw a line under the predicates.

Yes-No Questions

> **A *Yes-No question* asks for a yes or no answer.**
>
> <u>Yes-No question:</u> Have you been to Kansas? No.

There are many kinds of questions. Some take a long time to answer. The answer may need many words. Others can be answered quickly. You can say *yes* or *no*.

Look at these Yes-No questions.

> Have you been to Arkansas?
> Did you go in a car?

How would you answer the questions? You could say *yes* or *no*.

You can also turn a statement into a Yes-No question. These statements have been turned into questions.

> Jess is moving. → Is Jess moving?
> The van is ready. → Is the van ready?
> He will leave soon. → Will he leave soon?

Turn these sentences into Yes-No questions.

> Mary is living in Canada. She will visit us.

Can your questions be answered with *yes* or *no*?

PRACTICE

A. (Oral) Read the questions. Say the five Yes-No questions.

1. Are diamonds in Arkansas?
2. They sure are!
3. How can you find one?
4. Can you keep them?
5. Arkansas has more than diamonds.
6. It also has hot springs.
7. Is the water really hot?
8. It pours out of the ground.
9. Can you touch it?
10. Is there cold water also?

Yes.

Can you reach it?

B. (Written) Write the four Yes-No questions.

1. Are there mountains in Arkansas?
2. Are they the Boston Mountains?
3. Where are the Ozarks?
4. They are full of animals.
5. Tourists like the animals.
6. Why can't we stay longer?
7. Are there forests in Arkansas?
8. Did you see Fort Smith?

APPLY

Write two Yes-No questions about a place you would like to visit. Make sure your questions can be answered with *yes* or *no*.

WH-Questions

> **WH-questions begin with the words *who, what, when, where, why,* or *how.***
>
> WH-word: what   WH-question: What time is it?

Many questions cannot be answered with one word. They need more than a *yes* or *no* answer. Such questions may start with a WH-word. Most WH-words begin with *wh.*

Look at the Word Bank. Which WH-word does not begin with *wh?*

Look at these WH-questions.

> Who is Neil Armstrong?
> Why are spaceships so big?

Can you answer with *yes* or *no?* No. You must give a different kind of answer.

Read this news story.

> Alan Shepard was an astronaut. His spaceship was Freedom 7. The trip on May 5, 1961, was 302 miles long.

Here are two WH-questions that the story answers. What are two others?

> Who was Alan Shepard?
> How long was his flight?

WORD BANK

WH-words

who
what
when
where
why
how

PRACTICE

A. (Oral) Read the questions. Say the four WH-questions. Tell which words are WH-words.

> **Example:** Who first walked on the moon?
> **Who**

1. When did Neil Armstrong walk on the moon?
2. Was he with someone?
3. What was that person's name?
4. Where did they land?
5. Have you seen their pictures?
6. Who else walked on the moon?

B. (Written) Number your paper from *1* to *5*. Find the answer to each question. Write its letter next to the number of the question.

> **Example: 1. b**

1. Who was Nellie Bly?
2. When was she born?
3. What was her real name?
4. How quickly did she circle the globe?
5. Where did she begin?

   a. She started in New York City.
   b. She was a newspaper writer.
   c. She was born in 1867.
   d. It was Elizabeth Cochrane.
   e. Her trip took 72 days.

APPLY

Think of a famous person you would like to meet. Write two WH-questions you would ask.

Review the Basics II

A. Subjects

Write the subject of each sentence. The subject may be one word. It may be a group of words. *(pages 28–29)*

1. Good food is needed for good health.
2. Water is also needed.
3. Your body is more than half water.
4. Everyone needs water.
5. Many fruits are full of water.
6. Skim milk is almost all water.
7. Thirst keeps you healthy.
8. A thirsty person drinks water.

B. Predicates

Write the predicate of each sentence. *(pages 30–31)*

1. Sunflowers will grow quickly.
2. Many people grow them in their gardens.
3. The flowers turn to the sun.
4. Many different kinds grow.
5. Some people eat sunflower seeds.
6. Some sunflowers grow wild.
7. The roots of one sunflower grow big and fat.
8. The fat roots taste good.

C. Yes-No Questions
Write the five Yes-No questions. *(pages 32–33)*

1. Do you read names on cans?
2. What do they tell?
3. Are all food cans the same size?
4. Is your store near you?
5. Have you ever cooked?
6. What are the four food groups?
7. Can you plan good meals?
8. What do you enjoy?

D. WH-Questions
Write the six WH-questions. Underline the WH-word in each sentence you write. *(pages 34–35)*

1. Do you know first aid?
2. Why do you wash a cut?
3. What do you cover it with?
4. Are you careful?
5. Who helps you?
6. Where do you find help?
7. How do you make a call?
8. Do you know your address?
9. When do you use the telephone book?
10. Do you know the number for the police?

13 COMMUNICATING

Paragraphs

A *paragraph* is a group of sentences. The sentences are about one main idea. A *topic sentence* tells that main idea. The other sentences tell more about the main idea.

Look at this paragraph.

Many animals lay eggs. Birds lay eggs. Frogs and toads lay eggs. Turtles do, too.

What is the main idea? What is the topic sentence? The other sentences tell more about the main idea. They give *details*. What do the details tell you?

Each sentence in a paragraph should be about the main idea.

Look at this paragraph.

Plants need some things to grow. Plants need water. Plants need light. I got a plant for my aunt. Plants need food, too.

What sentence does not belong? Why?

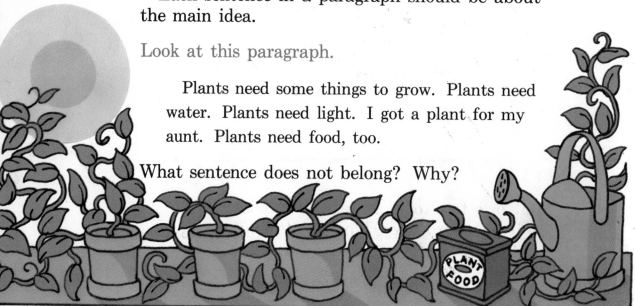

Notice that the first line of a paragraph is *indented*. It does not start all the way to the left.

The sentences should be in an order that makes sense. The next paragraph is mixed up.

Read the paragraph.

They can be used to make lumber. Trees are also used to make paper. Trees are useful in many ways.

How should the sentences be put in order? Tell the topic sentence first. Then put the detail sentences in an order that makes sense.

PRACTICE

(Written) Copy this paragraph. Underline the topic sentence. One sentence does not tell about the main idea. Draw a line through it.

Some animals are awake at night. They eat and play while we sleep. We need our sleep. Owls hunt at night. Bats hunt at night, too. Skunks are night animals, too.

APPLY

Below are two topic sentences. Choose one. Write it on your paper. Then write two sentences that tell more about the main idea.

Some games can be played indoors.
Many foods are red.

A Whole-Class Paragraph

You have learned that a paragraph is a group of sentences. They tell about one main idea. Now you will write a paragraph with your teacher.

First you will choose a topic. Some topics are too big for one paragraph. Is "food" a good topic? No. Writing about food would take more than one paragraph. Some part of that topic can be used. A paragraph can be about "food I ate today." It can be about "food I do not like."

Look at these topics.

animals
games
sports
buildings
tools
people
dogs
roller skating
weather

They are all too big for one paragraph. With your class, pick part of one topic for the paragraph.

Next you need a topic sentence. What do you want to say? What is the main idea? State it in a sentence. Your teacher will write it on the board.

A topic sentence is a good start. Now you need more sentences. They must tell more about the main idea.

Think of details. Your teacher will write them.

Are there any that do not tell about the main idea? Take them out. Are the details in an order that makes sense? If not, change the order.

Is the first line indented? Does each sentence begin and end correctly? If so, you have finished the paragraph.

PRACTICE

A. (Oral) Tell which three topics are not too big for a paragraph.

litter   jobs that I do

outdoor games   pollution

my favorite game   books

how to fly a kite   sports

animals on earth

stamps around the world

B. (Written) Choose one of the three topics from Practice A that are not too big for a paragraph. Write a topic sentence for it.

APPLY

Write a topic sentence about lunch or recess. Write another one about a pet you know.

A Paragraph: Plan, Write, Edit

By now, you know a lot about what makes a paragraph. You know that a topic sentence tells the main idea. You know that other sentences give details. The details must be in an order that makes sense.

Now you can write your own paragraph. You will plan it first. Then you will write it. Then you will edit it. Each step will help you to be a better writer.

PLAN

Look at the picture. What ideas does it give you? Think what you would like to tell about it.

The picture shows many people in a city. "The city" is not a good topic for a paragraph. It is too big. Choose something about the people in the city for your topic. Decide on your main idea.

What details do you notice? Write them down. Write as many as you can. Do not worry about the order yet. You are planning now.

WRITE

What steps must you take to write a good paragraph? There are some rules, or guidelines.

Read the Guidelines.

GUIDELINES

1. Be sure the topic is not too big.
2. Write a topic sentence.
3. Write detail sentences.

When you planned, you chose your topic. If it was not too big, you can now write a topic sentence. This will state the main idea. What is your main idea? Say it in a sentence.

Look at your list of details again. Check that each detail tells something about the main idea. Cross out any that do not.

Were your details just words or groups of words? If so, add to them now to make sentences.

Do your sentences make sense? Read them in different orders. Which order sounds best?

EDIT

Now you will edit your paragraph. When you edit, you look for mistakes and fix them. The Guidelines give some hints for this.

GUIDELINES

1. Indent the first line.
2. Start each sentence with a capital letter.
3. End each one with the right punctuation mark.
4. Fix any sentence that runs on.
5. Make sure each sentence is complete.
6. Check spelling. Use a dictionary for help.

Correct the next paragraph. Fix the sentence that runs on and on. There are three other errors.

Seeds come in many sizes. some are tiny. Carrot seeds are small. Apple and watermelon seeds are medium and there are also big seeds and a coconut is a big seed. It is so big that it hardly looks like a seed?

Now look at your own paragraph. Find any mistakes. Fix them. Use the Guidelines.

Copy your paragraph. Write as neatly as you can. You have made a paragraph that is special. It is all yours!

Listening for Information

There are many ways to learn. You can read new facts. You can see new sights. You can also listen.

Listen carefully. You will learn many things. Listening is important. When you practice, you get better. Listening well is a good habit to have.

Read the Guidelines.

GUIDELINES

1. Sit quietly.
2. Look at the speaker.
3. Listen for a topic sentence.
4. Listen for details.
5. Do not interrupt.
6. Save your questions for the end.

Use the Guidelines. You will become a better listener.

PRACTICE/APPLY

(Oral) Your teacher will read a paragraph aloud. Listen for the topic sentence. Listen for details, too. Can you remember them all?

Unit 1 Test

A. Sentences
Four groups of words are sentences. Two are not. Write the sentences. *(pages 10–11)*

1. Canada is larger than the United States.
2. It has many kinds of lands.
3. hilly lands and low mountains
4. Wide plains sweep across the center.
5. forests with thousands of lakes
6. In the far north, there are flat plains.

B. Beginning and Ending Sentences
Write each sentence correctly. Begin with a capital letter. End with the correct punctuation mark. *(pages 12–15)*

1. have you ever used a magnet
2. most magnets are made of iron
3. they put out a special force
4. it can pull or push
5. be careful

C. Subjects and Predicates
Write the subject of each sentence. *(pages 28–29)*

1. My sister Petra went to the library.
2. She wanted a book about ants.
3. Each room had shelves.
4. The shelves were full of books.

Write each predicate. *(pages 30–31)*

5. The man took Petra to the right room.
6. All the books were about science.
7. Petra found a book about insects.
8. She looked in the index.

D. Yes-No Questions and WH-Questions
Write the three Yes-No questions. *(pages 32–33)*

1. Have you ever painted a picture?
2. What did you paint?
3. Some people work as painters.
4. Do you know a painter?
5. Would you like to be one?

Write the four WH-questions. Underline the WH-words. *(pages 34–35)*

6. What is your favorite painting?
7. Did you paint it?
8. Where is it?
9. When was it painted?
10. What is it about?

E. Writing
Look at the picture on page 42. Choose a topic you have not written about. Write a paragraph that has a topic sentence and at least two detail sentences. *(pages 42–44)*

Something Extra

Writing on the Job

Marvin James is a cook. He makes all kinds of good things to eat. Marvin uses a form to write down the recipes for the things he makes. He keeps the recipes in a file so he will not lose them. Read the recipe on the next page.

What is the recipe for? The form gives two kinds of information. It tells the things the cook needs to have on hand. It tells the things the cook needs to do.

How many muffins can Marvin make with this recipe?

How many cups of flour would it take to make that many muffins?

Notice the details that Marvin included in his recipe. He told how much of each thing he needs. He told the steps in the correct order.

Write Away!

Pretend you are a cook. Your job is to make fruit salad for a hundred hungry people. Write a recipe for fruit salad. Use the same form that Marvin used. Tell what kinds of fruit you will put in it. List the things you will need to do in the right order.

You might want to use some of these things in your recipe. Add others of your own.

Fantastic Fruit Salad

30 ripe pineapples

13 honeydew melons

Chop the apples into small bits.

Mix all the fruit in a large bowl.

Marvin's Marvelous Muffin Mix (makes 120 muffins)

Things I need to get:	Things I need to do:
20 cups of flour	1. Heat the oven
20 tablespoons of sugar	2. Mix the flour, sugar, baking powder, and salt.
22 teaspoons of baking powder	3. Mix eggs, milk, and butter.
5 teaspoons of salt	4. Add the wet mixture to the dry mixture and stir.
10 eggs	
10 cups of milk	5. Pour into muffin tins.
4 cups of melted butter	6. Bake until done.

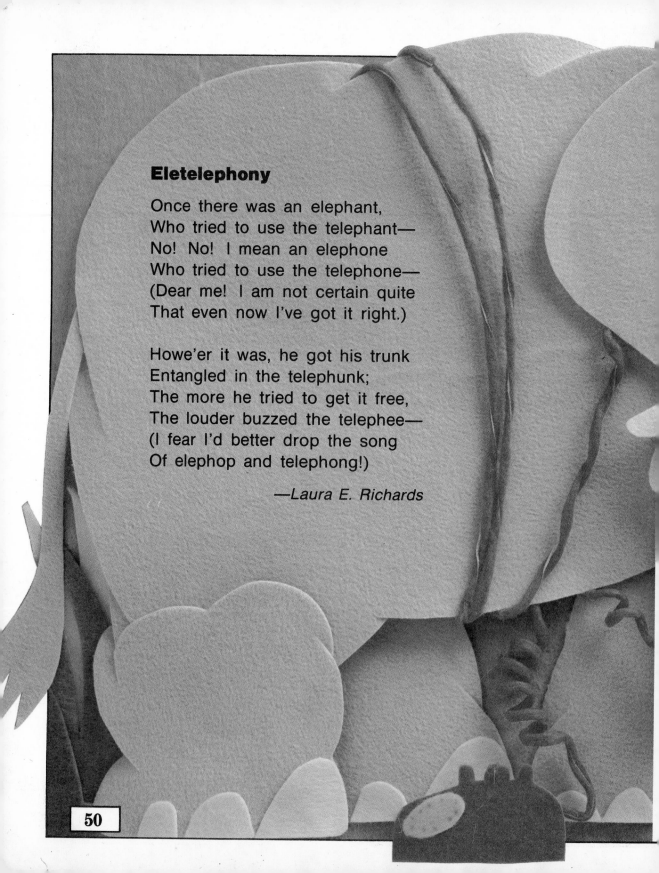

Eletelephony

Once there was an elephant,
Who tried to use the telephant—
No! No! I mean an elephone
Who tried to use the telephone—
(Dear me! I am not certain quite
That even now I've got it right.)

Howe'er it was, he got his trunk
Entangled in the telephunk;
The more he tried to get it free,
The louder buzzed the telephee—
(I fear I'd better drop the song
Of elephop and telephong!)

—*Laura E. Richards*

2

Giving
and Taking
Messages

SKILLS TO BUILD ON

Singular and Plural Nouns
Common and Proper Nouns
Possessive Nouns
Abbreviations
Commas

PRACTICAL APPLICATIONS

Writing an Invitation
Listening to Messages

Nouns

> **A *noun* is a word that names any person, place, or thing.**
>
> My <u>friend</u> at the <u>store</u> gave me a free <u>pen</u>.

People have different jobs. Words have different jobs, too. One job is to name something. A noun does this job. A *noun* names a person, place, or thing.

Look at these examples.

> **Person:** clown, aunt, neighbor, nurse
> **Place:** school, store, circus, kitchen
> **Thing:** hammer, rose, skunk, rain

Some nouns name one person, place, or thing. These are called *singular nouns.* Some nouns name more than one. These are called *plural nouns.*

Look at these nouns.

Singular→Plural		
teacher→teachers	boy→boys	girl→girls

What was added to make each noun plural?

PRACTICE

A. (Oral) Tell which words are nouns.

> **Example:** Wheat grew in the fields.
> **Wheat, fields**

1. Some farmers grow wheat.
2. Wheat can be made into flour.
3. A baker buys a sack of flour.
4. The baker makes bread.
5. The bread is baked in an oven.
6. The packages go to a store.
7. A person unloads the truck.

B. (Written) Complete each sentence with a noun.

> **Example:** The _____ was in the mailbox.
> **letter**

1. A _____ works outside.
2. A _____ works inside.
3. A _____ works in the country.
4. A _____ works in the city.
5. Some people work in a _____ .
6. Other people work in a _____ .
7. Some farmers grow _____ .
8. Some gardeners grow _____ .

APPLY

Think of people in a crowd. Write two sentences about them. Draw a line under each noun.

Plural Nouns

> **Plural nouns** are nouns that mean "more than one."
>
> tree→trees box→boxes

A *singular noun* names one person, place, or thing. A *plural noun* names more than one. Change the spelling of a singular noun to make it plural.

Read these words.

> job→jobs writer→writers book→books
> house→houses builder→builders nail→nails

Which of the nouns above are plural? To make many nouns plural, just add *-s*.

Now read these words.

> coach→coaches bush→bushes class→classes
> circus→circuses fox→foxes buzz→buzzes

The nouns above end with *ch, sh, ss, s, x,* and *zz.* To make such nouns plural, add *-es.*

In the next sentences, there are both singular and plural nouns. Which nouns are singular? Which are plural?

> **Builders** worked on the **house.**
> Two **brushes** were on the **floor.**
> The **paint** was dry in **minutes.**

PRACTICE

A. (Written) Write the plural form of each noun.

> **Example:** ladder
> **ladders**

1. letter	**4.** truck	**7.** tool	**10.** raccoon
2. friend	**5.** butcher	**8.** glass	**11.** house
3. dress	**6.** store	**9.** mix	**12.** wish

B. (Written) Write the plural form of each noun.

> **Example:** pilot
> **pilots**

13. sound	**15.** mess	**17.** wax	**19.** stitch
14. morning	**16.** dish	**18.** buzz	**20.** brush

APPLY

Think of people at work. Write two sentences about them. Use a plural noun in each sentence.

More Plural Nouns

> **There are different ways to form plural nouns.**
> ship→ships berry→berries ranch→ranches foot→feet

For many nouns you need to add *-s* to form the plural. For other nouns you need to add *-es.*

Read these words.

> tent→tents   place→places   box→boxes

Which nouns above are plural? To which noun was *-es* added? Remember, for nouns that end with *ch, sh, ss, s, x,* and *zz,* add *-es.*

Some nouns end with a consonant letter and the letter *y.*

Look at these words.

> baby→babies   pony→ponies   family→families

Which nouns above are plural? Do you see the spelling change? To make these nouns plural, change the *y* to *i* and add *-es.*

A few nouns must be changed in other ways. Some of these words are listed below. These plural nouns have special spellings. Memorize them.

> man→men   woman→women   child→children
> tooth→teeth   mouse→mice   goose→geese

PRACTICE

A. (Written) Write the plural form of each noun.

> **Example:** kitty
> **kitties**

1. party
2. woman
3. cherry
4. city
5. birthday
6. bunny
7. man
8. child
9. branch
10. tooth
11. penny
12. foot

B. (Written) Write the plural form of each noun.

> **Example:** bush
> **bushes**

13. goose
14. thought
15. uncle
16. blueberry
17. library
18. circus
19. butterfly
20. enemy
21. inch
22. mouse

APPLY

Think about watching baby animals at play. Write two sentences about them. Draw a line under each noun.

Common and Proper Nouns

> A *common noun* names any person, place, or thing. A *proper noun* is a special name.
>
> <u>Common noun:</u> girl   <u>Proper noun:</u> Marie

Proper nouns are special nouns. They are like the names we have for pets, streets, or states. Proper nouns begin with capital letters.

Your school has a special name. What is it? The name of your school is a proper noun. The word *school* is a *common noun*. The word *school* can mean any school.

Look at these common and proper nouns.

Common Nouns → Proper Nouns	
woman→Joan Miller	aunt→Aunt Linda
man→Alex Garza	cat→Fluff
uncle→Uncle Ken	school→Strand School

Name another proper noun for each common noun above.

Now read these sentences. Your special name for a parent is a proper noun.

We visited **Dad** at his office.
We met **Mom** for lunch.

PRACTICE

A. (Oral) Give a proper noun for each common noun.

> **Example:** aunt
> **Aunt Ana**

1. classmate
2. school
3. friend
4. parent
5. cat
6. grown-up
7. dog

B. (Written) Write the six proper nouns from this list.

1. sister
2. police officer
3. Officer Roth
4. Patches
5. Grandpa North
6. clerk
7. dentist
8. Brenda
9. kitten
10. aunt
11. Sterling School
12. John Byers

APPLY

Pretend you are meeting some friends. Write two sentences about this. Use as many proper nouns as you can.

More Proper Nouns

> A *proper noun* names a special person, place, or thing. It always begins with a capital letter.
>
> Common noun: state   Proper noun: Utah

The special name of a person is a *proper noun.* Special names of places or things are proper nouns, too. Remember that a proper noun begins with a capital letter.

Study the chart.

Proper Nouns

Names of Streets and Roads	Park Street Maple Lane Post Road Fifth Avenue
Names of Towns and Cities	Dallas Union San Diego New York City
Names of States	Texas California Ohio Vermont Idaho Florida
Names of Days of the Week	Sunday Thursday Friday
Names of Months	October March June
Names of Special Days	Valentine's Day Flag Day

PRACTICE

A. (Oral) Tell which nouns are proper nouns. Some sentences have more than one.

> **Example:** My father works in Portland.
> **Portland**

1. He works in the garden in May, June, July, and August.
2. We like living in Maine.
3. Our home is on Ivy Lane.
4. My father was born on a Monday.
5. My mother works in Boothbay.
6. She writes stories about Maine.
7. Her office is on Lincoln Street.
8. She works on Tuesday, Thursday, and Friday.

B. (Written) Find the seven proper nouns. Write them correctly.

> **Example:** bronxville
> **Bronxville**

1. august
2. evening
3. saturday
4. walnut street
5. hollywood
6. town
7. week
8. april fool's day
9. road
10. utah
11. friday
12. afternoon

APPLY

Where would you like to be on your favorite special day? Write two sentences about it. Use proper nouns.

Review the Basics I

A. Nouns

Write the nouns in each sentence. *(pages 52–53)*

1. My mother measures with a ruler.
2. The top of the table is clean.
3. My sister washed the dishes.
4. She used soap and water.
5. Ken brushed his teeth.
6. He put toothpaste on the brush.
7. His brother turned on the water.

B. Plural Nouns

Write the plural form of each noun. *(pages 54–55)*

1. hill
2. bush
3. mountain
4. kiss
5. lake
6. wood
7. beach
8. plane

Write the plural form of each noun. *(pages 56–57)*

9. wax
10. berry
11. river
12. child
13. city
14. puppy
15. goose
16. bus

C. Common and Proper Nouns
Write the nine proper nouns from this list.
(pages 58–59)

1. villages
2. Aunt Inez
3. Portland
4. New Year's Day
5. Perkins School
6. plumber
7. yesterday
8. Thursday
9. schoolhouse
10. Debra Powell
11. Uncle Wells
12. town line
13. vacation time
14. Puerto Rico
15. baseball player
16. time zone
17. game
18. Texas

D. More Proper Nouns
Find the eight proper nouns. Write them correctly. *(pages 60–61)*

1. garden city
2. brother
3. calendar
4. rhode island
5. fifth avenue
6. town
7. clerk
8. monday
9. youngstown
10. november
11. monthly
12. morning
13. bill miller
14. columbus day
15. day
16. state

Nouns in a Sentence

You often use nouns when you write sentences. You use common nouns or proper nouns. These name people, places, or things. You may use singular or plural nouns.

Read these sentences.

> A **pilot** flies **planes**.
> The **planes** land at the **airport**.

Each sentence above has one singular noun. Each one has one plural noun. Which nouns are singular? Which are plural?

Use a proper noun when you write about a special person, place, or thing. Proper nouns begin with capital letters. They often help make your meaning clear. The next two sentences use both kinds of nouns.

Look at these sentences.

> **Uncle Jay** is a **pilot**.
> He flew a **jet** last **Tuesday**.

How many proper nouns are in each sentence? Name them. What are the common nouns?

Nouns are important in sentences. Use them correctly. You will help your reader to understand your sentences.

PRACTICE/APPLY

A. (Written) Complete each sentence. Write either a singular or a plural noun for each.

Example: A _____ needs many workers.
city

1. It needs fire fighters and _____ .
2. It needs bus drivers and _____ .
3. What happens when a _____ needs help?
4. Someone might need a _____ .
5. What if a _____ is hungry?
6. Where can a person buy _____ ?
7. Grocers sell _____ .
8. Others make or sell _____ .
9. In parks you see _____ .

B. (Written) Find each proper noun. Write it correctly.

Example: She went to los angeles.
Los Angeles

10. carmen wanted a job with animals.
11. On sunday she called some people.
12. One place needed help each monday.
13. A pet store on main street needed help.
14. One animal doctor was named paula smith.
15. She wanted help in august.
16. One dog was named freckles.
17. uncle jake knew the dog's owner.
18. Now Carmen works in lawndale.

Abbreviations

Abbreviations are short, quick ways to write some words. Most end with periods. Abbreviations for proper nouns start with capital letters.

Some people use titles with their names. Look at these abbreviations for titles.

any man→Mr.   a married woman→Mrs.
any woman→Ms.   a doctor→Dr.

The days of the week have short forms. The names of most months do, too.

Look at the Word Bank.

Three months do not have abbreviations. They are May, June, and July. Why do you think they are not shortened?

Names of streets have short forms, too.

Main Street → Main St.
Grand Avenue → Grand Ave.
Hill Road → Hill Rd.

Notice that only one word in each name has an abbreviation. Which word has an abbreviation?

Names of states have two abbreviations. One form looks more like the name of the state. The other form is the postal abbreviation. It is used for the mail. It must be followed by a ZIP Code.

WORD BANK	
Days	
Sun.	Thurs.
Mon.	Fri.
Tues.	Sat.
Wed.	
Months	
Jan.	Sept.
Feb.	Oct.
Mar.	Nov.
Apr.	Dec.
Aug.	

Here are the abbreviations for several states. Do you know your state's abbreviation?

Abbreviations for States

State	Abbreviation	Postal Abbreviation
Arizona	Ariz.	AZ
California	Calif.	CA
Texas	Tex.	TX

PRACTICE

A. (Written) Write the abbreviations for the underlined words.

Examples: California   Main Street
Calif. or CA   **St.**

1. Devon Road
2. Rollins Street
3. Doctor Lang
4. Texas
5. Tuesday
6. North Avenue
7. March
8. Saturday

B. (Written) Write the abbreviations for these words.

9. December
10. Arizona
11. Friday
12. Sunday
13. Monday
14. August
15. April
16. Wednesday
17. October

APPLY

Write the abbreviations for today's day and month. Write the abbreviation for your state.

Using Commas

A *comma* (,) is a punctuation mark. It is used in many places. Use a comma with dates. Put the comma between the day and the year.

Look at these examples.

July 2, 1984
June 6, 1970
April 14, 1937

Also use a comma in a list of three or more words in a sentence.

Find the commas in these sentences.

Andrew, Inez, and Mako are in the third grade.
Andrew likes reading, writing, and science.
Inez likes art, math, music, and reading.
Mako likes music and science.

There is no comma in the last sentence. Why?

The commas are missing in these sentences. Where should the commas be added?

Aunt Marcie was born on March 31 1963.
She likes to read fish and run.

PRACTICE

A. (Written) Write each date correctly. Add punctuation marks. Use capital letters if they are needed.

Example: april 16 1982
April 16, 1982

1. April 26 1930
2. July 19 1954
3. August 6 1904
4. february 11 1873
5. january 20 1975
6. October 8 1911
7. December 23 1928
8. may 13 1981
9. September 7 1860
10. november 10 1807
11. march 15 1919
12. june 30 1976

B. (Written) Write each sentence correctly. Put commas where they belong.

Example: We grow grapes pears and plums.
We grow grapes, pears, and plums.

13. Eyes can be blue brown or green.
14. The pet shop sold fish birds and kittens.
15. Maura Tim and I went skating.
16. Ralph likes to sing ride and dance.
17. Becky found a penny a dime and a book.

APPLY

Suppose you were shopping for food today. Write one sentence using today's date. Write another about four foods you will buy. Put the commas where they are needed.

Capitals and Commas in Letters

You know how to use commas in dates. They go between the day and the year. You also know that they go between words in a list.

Commas are used in other ways, too. Use a comma between city and state names. Use one after a friendly letter greeting. Use a comma after the closing.

See how commas are used in this letter.

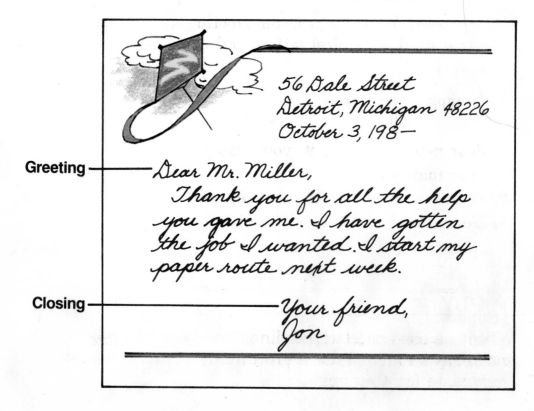

Greeting

Closing

> 56 Dale Street
> Detroit, Michigan 48226
> October 3, 198—
>
> Dear Mr. Miller,
>   Thank you for all the help you gave me. I have gotten the job I wanted. I start my paper route next week.
>
>   Your friend,
>   Jon

PRACTICE

A. (Written) Write each letter heading correctly. Use capital letters and commas where needed.

Example: 258 george street   **258 George Street**
Fairfax, Virginia 22030   **Fairfax, Virginia 22030**
May 25 1984   **May 25, 1984**

1. 17 pine street
Troy New York 12180
March 25, 1974

3. 28 marion street
Sitka alaska 99835
february 14 1978

2. 263 Lowry Road
rome, Georgia 30161
june 18 1952

4. 53 syre Avenue
Chicago Illinois 60611
april 12, 1981

B. (Written) Write each letter greeting and closing correctly. Use capital letters and commas where needed.

Example: your classmate   **Your classmate,**
allen   **Allen**

5. dear ned

6. dear marilyn

7. dear sue

8. Your friend
anna

9. yours truly
José

10. sincerely
Ralph

APPLY

Write a correct letter heading. Use your address and today's date. Write a greeting to a friend. Use your name for a closing.

Using *A, An,* and *The*

> ***Articles*** **are small words that mark nouns. The words *a, an,* and *the* are articles.**
>
> <u>a</u> book   <u>an</u> author   <u>the</u> store

Nouns have one job. You know that they name people, places, or things. *Articles* have another job. Articles mark nouns. When you see *a, an,* or *the,* a noun is coming.

Look at these sentences.

> Eva wrote **a** report. She used **an** atlas.
> **The** maps were helpful.

Name the articles in the sentences. What noun follows each one?

Use *a* or *an* with a singular noun. Use *an* before a word that begins with a vowel sound. The article *the* may be used with all nouns, singular or plural.

Look at these examples.

> Eva wrote **a** good report.
> Ben wrote about **an** artist.
> Carlo drew **the** pictures.

Most of the nouns are singular. Which article can be used with plural nouns? When are *a* and *an* used?

PRACTICE

A. (Oral) Tell the articles and their nouns.

> **Example:** An almanac is a book.
> **An—almanac, a—book**

1. The book has many facts.
2. An almanac tells the birthdays of famous people.
3. It has a list of special days.
4. The pages about sports are good.
5. The teams are listed.
6. The almanac tells about the states.
7. It has a list of the lakes.
8. An almanac has an index.

B. (Written) Write the correct article.

> **Example:** Our town has (a/an) library.
> **a**

1. I have (a/an) card for the library.
2. There is (a/an) room of magazines.
3. All (the/a) papers are there, too.
4. One room has (a/an) wall of pictures.
5. I look for (the/an) books by Peter Spier.
6. He is (a/an) artist.
7. He is (a/an) author, too.
8. Look at (a/an) picture.

APPLY

What do you like about books? Write two sentences about books. Begin each with an article.

Singular Possessive Nouns

> A *possessive noun* is a noun that shows who
> or what owns or has something.
>
> <u>Singular possessive</u>: the girl's game

A *possessive noun* is a short way to show
possession. *Possession* means that a person or
living thing has or owns something. Something
belongs to a person or living thing.

You can show possession by writing a group of
words. You can show it by writing one word. That
word is a *possessive noun*.

Look at the examples.

> the pen of the writer → the **writer's** pen
> the boat the sailor has → the **sailor's** boat
> the cap the nurse has → the **nurse's** cap

The word *writer's* is a singular possessive noun. So
are the words *sailor's* and *nurse's*. Each word ends
with *'s*. The mark before *s* is an *apostrophe*.

Remember, form the possessive of most singular
nouns by adding *'s*.

Say these groups of words in a shorter way.

> the book of the author
> the arm the pitcher has
> the flippers of the diver

PRACTICE

A. (Written) Show possession using fewer words.
Write possessive nouns.

Example: the paws the cat has
the cat's paws

1. the book the boy has
2. the smile of the girl
3. the job that Nana has
4. the radio the man owns

5. the laugh that Ellen has
6. the boots of the farmer
7. the courage of Kelly
8. the kite that Joe has

B. (Written) Write each sentence. Use fewer
words for the underlined words. Use possessive
nouns.

Example: The smile that Eric has is cheerful.
Eric's smile is cheerful.

9. Eric sat in the office of Dr. Hill.
10. Dr. Hill cleaned the teeth Eric has.
11. Eric took a cup from the hand of the nurse.
12. Meg marked the chart the doctor owns.
13. The teeth the boy has are fine.
14. The dentist fixed a tooth that Mother has.
15. The toothbrush Eric has is blue.

APPLY

What do you notice when you see the doctor or
dentist? Write two sentences about things the
doctor has or owns. Use possessive nouns.

Plural Possessive Nouns

> **A plural noun may show possession.**
>
> <u>Plural possessive</u>: students' papers

A possessive noun can be singular or plural. You learned about singular ones in Lesson 11. You make singular nouns possessive by adding *'s*.

In this lesson you will learn how to make *plural possessive nouns*. They are made in two ways.

Read these rules.

Plural Possessive Nouns

Some plural nouns end with _s_. Add only the apostrophe.
the dogs the girls own→the **girls'** dogs
Some plural nouns do not end with _s_. Add _'s_.
the jobs the women have→the **women's** jobs

If *one* girl had two dogs, where would the apostrophe go?

Now look at these possessive nouns.

sisters' baby's turtles' birds' farmer's

Which are singular? Which are plural? Notice the ways they are formed.

PRACTICE

A. (Oral) What is the possessive noun in each sentence? Tell if it is *singular* or *plural*.

> **Example:** The mothers' voices stopped.
> **mothers'—plural**

1. The girls' mittens felt damp.
2. The birds' songs were pretty.
3. The child's boots were wet.
4. My uncle's store opens at noon.
5. The children's hands were clean.
6. The boy's crayons were broken.
7. The puppy's fur was soft.

B. (Written) Show possession using fewer words. Write possessive nouns.

> **Example:** the food of the dogs
> **the dogs' food**

1. the bells the boys have
2. the wings of the insects
3. the music the singers own
4. the jobs the women have
5. the shells the turtles have
6. the tickets the fans own

APPLY

Write one sentence about rabbits. Write one about clowns. Use a plural possessive noun in each.

Review the Basics II

A. Using *A, An,* and *The*
Write the correct article for each sentence.
(pages 72–73)

1. A baby cow is (a/an) calf.
2. (A/An) elephant has a calf, too.
3. (A/An) elk baby is also called a calf.
4. (The/A) bears all have cubs.
5. A baby tiger is also (a/an) cub.
6. A baby owl is (a/an) owlet.
7. (A/An) antelope has a kid.
8. (A/An) goat also has a kid.
9. A sheep has (a/an) lamb.
10. You know what has (a/an) kitten.
11. You know what has (a/an) puppy, too.

B. Singular Possessive Nouns
Show possession using fewer words. Write possessive nouns. *(pages 74–75)*

1. the fish the man has
2. the student the teacher has
3. the fields the farmer has
4. the shells the girl has
5. the pool my cousin owns
6. the summer the boy had
7. the hobby the girl has
8. the letter that Pam owns

C. Plural Possessive Nouns

Show possession using fewer words. Write possessive nouns. *(pages 76–77)*

1. the paper the boys have
2. the eggs of the chickens
3. the nuts the squirrels have
4. the dens the bears have
5. the nests of the birds
6. the tents of the campers
7. the fuel the families have
8. the job of the workers

D. Singular and Plural Possessive Nouns

Number your paper from *1* to *8*. Write the possessive noun. *Write S* if the possessive noun is singular. Write *P* if it is plural. *(pages 74–77)*

1. The children's puppets have strings.
2. Many men's hats blew away.
3. The child's day was happy.
4. The dogs' dishes were full.
5. My sister's tooth is loose.
6. The duck's quack is funny.
7. The teachers' room is there.
8. The cat's purr was gentle.

Messages

Have you ever given someone a message? Perhaps you were telling about a phone call. Perhaps you were writing about a party. Giving a good message is important. You must tell all the facts.

Suppose you are giving a message. How can you make sure you tell all the facts? Remember the WH-questions. Remember *who, what, where, when, why,* and *how.* Your message should answer these questions. Then it will be clear.

Janet found this note on the kitchen table.

Read the note.

> Dear Janet,
>   Your softball coach called. You are invited to a meeting. It is at her house tonight at 7:00. It is about the team's name. I'll give you a ride.
>   Love,
>   Mom

Janet's mother wrote a good message. All the WH-questions are answered. The first sentence tells *whom* the message is from. The second sentence tells *what.* The third tells *where* and *when.* The fourth tells *why.* The fifth sentence tells *how.*

PRACTICE

A. (Oral) These messages are not complete. Add facts to make them clear.

> **Example:** Your classmate wants to play. Meet her at her house.
> **Sara called. Meet her at four o'clock.**

1. Your friend is coming over. He has a question about homework.
2. Jamie called. She said to call back after her supper.
3. Meet Tom at school tomorrow. Bring your book.

B. (Written) Someone put this note on Tony's desk. What WH-questions are not answered? Rewrite the note. Add the missing information.

Dear Tony,
Please be sure to watch Channel 1. I will be on the Kids News Show. I will talk about my pet skunk. I won the contest for the most unusual pet.
Your friend,

APPLY

When might you need to write messages? Write two sentences telling *when*.

Letters of Invitation

Suppose you are having a party. You may write an *invitation*. In it, you ask people to come. An invitation is like a message. You need to tell the facts. You need to answer WH-questions.

An invitation has five parts. They are the *heading, greeting, body, closing,* and *signature.*

Look at this invitation.

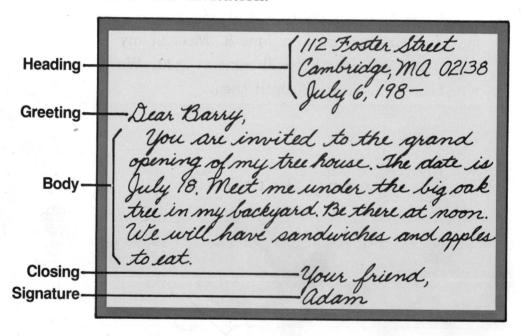

Heading
> 112 Foster Street
> Cambridge, MA 02138
> July 6, 198—

Greeting
> Dear Barry,

Body
> You are invited to the grand opening of my tree house. The date is July 18. Meet me under the big oak tree in my backyard. Be there at noon. We will have sandwiches and apples to eat.

Closing
> Your friend,

Signature
> Adam

The *heading* gives the address of the person who is writing. It tells the date. The *greeting* is a way to say hello. The *body* gives the facts. The *closing* is a way to say good-bye. The *signature* is the name of the person who wrote the letter.

PRACTICE

(Written) The parts of this letter are mixed up. Write the letter. Put the parts in the right order.

Your friend,
Laura

366 Sixth Ave.
New York City, NY 10003
June 1, 198—

Jeff's birthday is on June 9. I will have a surprise party for him on June 8. Meet at my apartment at 2:00. Jeff will come at 2:30. We will hide in the kitchen until then.

Dear Sara,

I hope you can come. Don't tell Jeff.

APPLY

Imagine you went to Jeff's party. Write two sentences about it.

An Invitation:
Plan, Write, Edit

An invitation is like a message. You must tell all the facts. An invitation should tell *who, what, where,* and *when.* It may also tell *why* or *how.*

PLAN

This invitation has five parts. It has a *heading, greeting,* and *body.* It has a *closing* and *signature.*

Read the invitation.

35 Star Road
Butler, NJ 07405
February 11, 198—

Dear Robin,
    You are invited to a toy sale. The date is February 22. The sale will start at noon. It will be held at school. It will end at 4:00. There will be dolls. There will be board games. There will also be bikes.
    The money will go to the Wheelchair Fund. This will help a child from our town.
                    Your friend,
                    Randy

Think of an invitation you want to write. Write it for one of these events.

a surprise party   a used-book sale
a lemonade-stand opening   a skating party

Write notes. Your list of notes might look like these.

Read the notes.

Who: Maria and John
What: come to a picnic
Where: Brookside Picnic Grounds
When: May 25 at 1:00 P.M.

WRITE

Write your invitation. Include the five parts of a letter. Remember the heading and greeting. Write the body. Answer WH-questions. Your friend does not know about the event. You must tell the facts. Do not forget the closing. Sign your name.

Use the Guidelines.

GUIDELINES

1. An invitation has five parts. It has a heading greeting, and body. It has a closing and signature.
2. An invitation answers WH-questions. It must say *who, what, where,* and *when.* It may also say *why* and *how.*

EDIT

Now you are ready to edit. Check for capital letters. Check punctuation marks. Look for WH-answers. Practice on this invitation. Find the mistakes and fix them. Rewrite the letter.

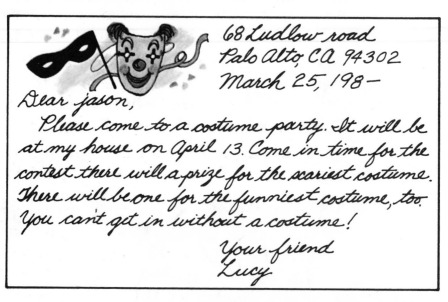

68 Ludlow road
Palo Alto, CA 94302
March 25, 198—

Dear jason,

Please come to a costume party. It will be at my house on April 13. Come in time for the contest there will a prize for the scariest costume. There will be one for the funniest costume, too. You can't get in without a costume!

Your friend
Lucy

Now edit your own work. Use the Guidelines.

GUIDELINES

1. Check the five letter parts.
2. Answer the WH-questions in the body.
3. Use capital letters correctly.
4. Check punctuation marks.

Editing is important. Fix mistakes you find. Check that your writing makes sense. Copy your letter in your best handwriting.

Listening to Messages

Listening to messages is important. Listen carefully. Remember the answers to WH-questions. If you do not listen, you may forget some facts.

One way to remember a message is to take notes. Do not write everything. Answer only the WH-questions. They are *who, what, where, when, why,* and *how.* Then you will have all the facts.

Listen carefully. Your teacher will read some messages. Listen for answers to WH-questions.

PRACTICE/APPLY

(Oral) Listen to the messages. Take notes on each one. Make sure your notes answer WH-questions. Then your teacher will ask you to tell the messages.

Unit 2 Test

A. Nouns
Write the nouns in each sentence. *(pages 52–53)*

1. One city has a famous grasshopper.
2. The insect is on a building.
3. This insect turns in the wind.
4. The grasshopper is a weather vane.
5. Winds push the grasshopper.
6. It shows how the wind is blowing.
7. Some people collect these vanes.
8. Look for pictures of them in books.

B. Plural Nouns
Write the plural form of each noun. *(pages 54–57)*

1. ax	**4.** switch	**7.** foot	**10.** toy
2. chair	**5.** lace	**8.** party	**11.** loss
3. rug	**6.** paper	**9.** sock	**12.** push

C. Proper Nouns
Find each proper noun. Write it correctly. *(pages 58–61)*

1. In october of 1869, some people were digging.
2. They found a stone giant in new york.
3. The land was near the town of cardiff.
4. william newell, the owner, put up a tent.
5. His cousin george sold tickets.

D. Using *A*, *An*, and *The*

Write the correct article for each sentence.
(pages 72–73)

1. Lillian Leitzel was (a/an) acrobat.
2. Her mother was (a/an) performer, too.
3. Her grandmother swung on (a/an) trapeze at 80.
4. Lillian worked with (a/an) circus.
5. (The/A) muscles in her arms were strong.
6. She wore (a/an) cape and gold shoes.
7. She took (a/an) piano with her.
8. She became (a/an) star.

E. Possessive Nouns

Show possession using fewer words. Write possessive nouns. *(pages 74–77)*

1. the jacket that Pat owns
2. the shirt Sal has
3. the clothes of the children
4. the bats the boys have
5. the mitts the girls own
6. the hat the man has
7. the cheers of the crowd
8. the prize of the team

F. Writing

Write an invitation to a party. Use all letter parts. Write the heading and greeting. Use your address and today's date in the heading. Write the body. Give the important facts. Remember to use a closing. End with your name. *(pages 84–86)*

Keep Practicing

A. Sentences
Four groups of words are sentences. Four are not. Write the sentences. *(Unit 1, Lesson 1)*

1. eating curds and whey
2. Curds come from milk.
3. Many cheeses are made from curds.
4. some of the best cheeses
5. Cheese is rich in protein.
6. sprinkled with chopped herbs
7. Some cheese is green.
8. in many good recipes

B. Kinds of Sentences
Number your paper from *1* to *8*. Read each sentence. Write *S* if it is a statement. Write *Q* if it is a question. Write *E* if it is an exclamation. *(Unit 1, Lesson 2)*

1. What is Amalia making?
2. It is delicious!
3. Amalia is a good cook.
4. You tasted her fruit salad.
5. How many fruits are in it?
6. She used apples, pears, grapes, and oranges.
7. May I please have some more?
8. I love it, too!

C. Subjects

Write the subject of each sentence. The subject may be one word. It may be a group of words. *(Unit 1, Lesson 9)*

1. Emily is growing a tree.
2. A seed started it.
3. The little grapefruit was planted.
4. The soil was watered.
5. Leaves appeared quickly.
6. More and more leaves grew.
7. Each leaf was shiny.
8. The grapefruit tree likes sunshine.

D. Predicates

Write the predicate of each sentence. *(Unit 1, Lesson 10)*

1. Many old quilts are beautiful.
2. They are made from pieces of cloth.
3. A great many people have quilted.
4. Quilts keep people warm.
5. Quilts used up tiny scraps.
6. Some quilters followed patterns.
7. Each small piece was carefully cut.
8. Beautiful quilts are still made today.

E. Yes-No Questions and WH-Questions

Write the four Yes-No questions. *(Unit 1, Lesson 11)*

1. Is that a redwood?
2. Why is it so big?
3. Will we see more?
4. Are we driving through a tree?
5. When was the tree planted?
6. Have you got the camera?
7. Where will you send the pictures?
8. How many pictures do you have?

Write the seven WH-questions. Underline the WH-word in each sentence you write. *(Unit 1, Lesson 12)*

9. How do you write a secret message?
10. What do you write it with?
11. Where do you get lemon juice?
12. Why does vinegar work so well?
13. Are you using juice instead of ink?
14. Who showed you this trick?
15. Is it invisible when it is dry?
16. When will you warm the paper?
17. How does a lightbulb make the message brown?
18. That is a good idea you have!

F. Beginning and Ending Sentences
Write each sentence correctly. *(Unit 1, Lesson 3)*

1. How can I find Julius Lester's book
2. first, go to the library.
3. Ask where the fiction is kept
4. Those books are arranged by author
5. their last names are in alphabetical order.
6. which book did you want

G. Parts of a Book
Number your paper from *1* to *6*. Write *T* if the sentence is true. Write *F* if it is false. *(Unit 1, Lesson 7)*

1. The title appears on the cover.
2. The contents can be called the "table of contents."
3. The contents are in alphabetical order.
4. In the back of some books is an index.
5. The index lists subjects in alphabetical order.
6. The index only lists names of people.

H. Alphabetical Order
Write each group of words in alphabetical order. *(Unit 1, Lesson 6)*

1. life, love, lunch
2. paper, pound, pepper
3. cotton, cat, cent
4. matches, money, meat
5. bed, bottles, baby
6. fire, farm, food
7. house, hut, hill
8. friend, family, fur

Poetry in Motion

What is a poem? Here is one that talks about a poem.

A poem is a worm sneaking along the wet grass wiggling toward the green of an APPLE!

How can a poem be a worm? In a way, poems are like worms. They sneak around things. They wiggle with words. They capture things. They like to be inside things.

Here is another poem. This poem captures a bird. What does the bird capture?

A bird came down the walk:
He did not know I saw;
He bit an angle-worm in halves
And ate the fellow, raw.
—Emily Dickinson

Poems come in many shapes. Some have plain shapes. The poem about the bird has a plain shape. Other poems have strange shapes.

Read the first poem again. Follow the words (and the worm). Turn your book as you read. This poem is a *concrete poem*. Concrete poems have actions shapes. They look and act like the subject of the poem. This poem acts like a wiggly worm and looks like an apple. Can you think of a title for the poem?

Write Away!

Write a concrete poem. Use one of the things below as the subject of your poem. Think of a shape for your poem. Then write the poem in that shape.

snake	pumpkin	telephone pole	wishbone
glasses	pine tree	flag	ocean waves

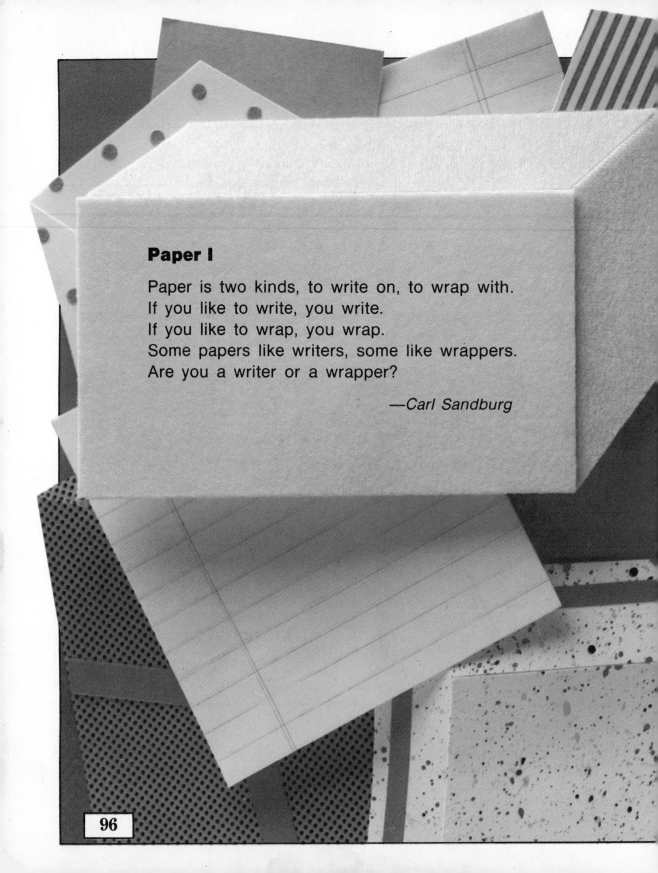

Paper I

Paper is two kinds, to write on, to wrap with.
If you like to write, you write.
If you like to wrap, you wrap.
Some papers like writers, some like wrappers.
Are you a writer or a wrapper?

—*Carl Sandburg*

3

Writing
Letters

SKILLS TO BUILD ON

Verbs and Verb Tenses
Subject-Verb Agreement
Irregular Verbs
Directions

PRACTICAL APPLICATIONS

Writing a Business Letter
Making Introductions

Action Verbs

> An *action verb* shows what someone or something does.
>
> Maria|<u>swims</u> in the pond.

Every sentence needs a *verb.*

Look at these sentences.

Kim|**eats** lunch.   Pat|**walks** to school.

The action verbs are *eats* and *walks.* What are the action verbs in these sentences?

Kim rides her bike. Pat sees her.

PRACTICE

(Written) Write the nine action verbs.

1. bakes
2. throws
3. heavy
4. loud
5. laughs
6. reads
7. writes
8. quickly
9. sad
10. swims
11. falls
12. yellow
13. speaks
14. lifts
15. happy

APPLY

Write two sentences about you. Use action verbs.

Other Verbs

> A *verb* may tell what someone or something is, was, or will be.
>
> Carlos|<u>is</u> my friend.   That joke|<u>was</u> funny.

Another kind of verb may show no action.

Look at the verbs in these sentences.

The sun|**is** bright.   The baby|**was** sleepy.

The verbs *is* and *was* do not show action.

PRACTICE

(**Written**) Write five verbs that do not show action.

Example: Iris is nine years old.
        is

1. We make apple rings.
2. Sam washed them.
3. He was quick.
4. Iris cuts the apples.
5. They tie on strings.
6. They will be in the sun.
7. They are dry.
8. Sam eats them.
9. Rings are a treat.
10. They were good.

APPLY

Write two sentences about apples. Use verbs that do not tell an action. Circle them.

Present Tense

> **A verb that names an action now is in the *present time,* or *tense.***
>
> **The sun <u>shines</u> brightly today.**

Verbs can show actions in the present. These verbs are in the present time, or tense.

We **grow** trees. Beth **picks** fruit.

Which verb ends in *s*? This is called the *s-form.* Use the *s*-form with subjects that mean *he, she,* and *it.*

Study the chart.

Forming the *s*-form of Verbs

For most verbs, add -s.	Some verbs end with *ch, sh, s, x,* or *zz.* Add *-es.*	Some verbs end with a consonant letter and *y.* Change the *y* to *i* and add *-es.*
pulls shouts	watches mixes pushes buzzes misses	cries worries

Do not use the *s*-form with subjects that mean *you* or *I* or with plural subjects.

You **hold** it. I **run** fast. We **watch**.

PRACTICE

A. (Oral) Find the subject of each sentence. Tell the correct present tense verb for each sentence.

> **Example:** We (love/loves) our new pets.
> **We love**

1. Our cat Tootsie (carry/carries) her kittens to her bed.
2. The kittens (box/boxes) Tootsie's ears.
3. Tootsie (hiss/hisses) if you go near her kittens.
4. My sister Amy (try/tries) to squeeze them.
5. She (rushes/rush) to see them every morning.
6. Dad (look/looks) at them, too.
7. Amy (like/likes) the kittens' soft fur.
8. It (feel/feels) like velvet.

B. (Written) Write the present tense for each verb.

> **Example:** The baby (smack) her lips after she eats.
> **smacks**

1. A bee (fly) around the flower.
2. Some nights we (watch) the sunset.
3. Jimmy (mix) cereal and nuts for a snack.
4. If a bee (buzz) around you, stay still.
5. I (wish) that rain tasted like lemonade.
6. My dog Ralph (chase) his own tail.
7. My sister (miss) me.

APPLY

Think of an unusual animal. Write two sentences about it. Use verbs in the present tense.

Past Tense

> **A verb that tells about the past is in the *past tense*.**
>
> **Last night they <u>watched</u> TV.**

Present tense verbs name actions that are happening now. Other verbs tell about the past. These verbs are in the *past tense*.

Look at this sentence.

Yesterday Casey **walked** to school.

The verb *walked* is in the past tense.

Forming the Past Tense of Verbs

For most verbs, add *-ed*.	pull→pulled lift→lifted
Some verbs end with a final *e*. Drop the *e* and add *-ed*.	pile→piled wipe→wiped
Some verbs end with a single letter vowel followed by a single final consonant. Double the final consonant and add *-ed*.	chop→chopped rip→ripped
Some verbs end with a consonant letter and *y*. Change the *y* to *i* and add *-ed*.	marry→married worry→worried

PRACTICE

A. (Oral) Tell the verb that is in the past tense for each sentence.

> **Example:** Gino (<u>dressed</u>/dress) quickly.
> **dressed**

1. Gino (<u>hurried</u>/hurry) to school.
2. He (<u>walked</u>/walk) quickly to the corner.
3. At the red light, he (stop/<u>stopped</u>).
4. Then he (<u>waited</u>/wait) for the light to change.
5. Finally, the light (turn/<u>turned</u>) green.
6. Gino (<u>looked</u>/look) both ways.
7. He safely (cross/<u>crossed</u>) the street.

B. (Written) Write the past tense of each verb.

> **Example:** He (look) for the book.
> **looked**

1. Jerome (open) the cookbook.
2. He (try) the recipe for juice cubes.
3. First he (wash) some ice cube trays.
4. Then he (squeeze) the oranges.
5. He (pour) the juice into the trays.
6. He (drop) one toothpick into each cube.
7. He (push) the trays into the freezer.

APPLY

Suppose you walked a dog. A cat ran in front of you. Write two sentences about what happened. Use verbs in the past tense.

Future Tense

> **A verb may tell about something in the future. A verb that tells about the future is in the** *future tense.*
>
> **Next week they <u>will fix</u> the bike.**

You often talk about the future. You make plans. You expect some things to happen. For example, you know that school will be open on school days. Use the *future tense* to write about the future.

Look at these sentences.

> Tomorrow I **will buy** a kite.
> Dad **will take** me shopping.
> Next weekend the new park **will open.**

The verbs are in the future tense. One way to form the future tense is to use *will* with the verb. Use *will* to show that the action is in the future.

Find the future tense verbs in these sentences.

> Next Saturday we will fly the kite.
> We will tie a long tail on it.
> The wind will carry it up high.
> We will have a great day.
> Flying a kite is fun!

PRACTICE

A. (Oral) Tell the four verbs in the future tense.

> **Example:** My friend will travel to New Mexico.
> **will travel**

1. We lived in Georgia for a year.
2. We had a house on Elm Street.
3. I will show you my jumping beans.
4. They will jump in my hand.
5. They are warm now.
6. We will watch them.
7. A little worm is inside each bean.
8. The worm will become a moth.

B. (Written) Write the future tense of each verb.

> **Example:** Mom (runs) her best race of all.
> **will run**

1. The road race (begins) at Elm Park.
2. Mom (joins) me in the race.
3. We (join) other runners there.
4. Runners (stretch) their legs before a race.
5. When they do this, they (feel) better.
6. I (feel) good after I run.
7. Many children my age (run) in this race.

APPLY

What game or sport would you like to play in the future? Write two sentences telling what you will do. Use the future tense.

Review the Basics I

A. Verbs

Write the verb in each sentence. *(pages 98–99)*

1. Karen washes the car.
2. Mrs. Shay pays her.
3. She gives Karen one dollar.
4. Karen runs to the store.
5. Karen buys a box of pencils.
6. The pencils are many colors.
7. Karen pays sixty cents for them.
8. The salesperson takes the dollar.
9. He hands Karen the change.
10. The change is hers.

B. Present Tense

Write the present tense form of each verb.
(pages 100–101)

1. Nellie (need) a phone number.
2. She (wish) to call a taxi.
3. Nellie (find) the book in the kitchen.
4. She (carry) it to the hall.
5. Nellie (use) the Yellow Pages.
6. She (look) for the word taxicab.
7. She (hurry) because she is late.
8. Nellie says, "I (see) the number I need."

C. Past Tense

Write the past tense of each verb. *(pages 102–103)*

1. Bud (show) the class a trick.
2. He (carry) a pan with a cover.
3. He (lift) the lid.
4. An egg (float) on water.
5. Then Bud (pour) the water out.
6. He (fill) the pan with water again.
7. He (hand) the egg to the teacher.
8. The teacher (try) to make the egg float.
9. The egg (drop) to the bottom of the pan.
10. We (ask) Bud how he did it.
11. Bud (add) lots of salt to his water.

D. Future Tense

Write the future tense of each verb. *(pages 104–105)*

1. I (show) that seeds like warm soil.
2. We (fill) two pots with dirt.
3. Then Debra (open) the bag of seeds.
4. She (plant) four seeds in each pot.
5. One pot (go) on the warm window sill.
6. We (put) the other in the cold hall.
7. We (water) both pots.
8. The warm seeds (sprout) first.

Verbs in a Paragraph

When you write a paragraph, you use many verbs. You may use the present tense. You may use the past or future tense.

Look at the verbs in this paragraph.

Susie **knows** an old mouse. I **laughed** at
him. He **looks** so young! I **guessed** his name.
It **is** Mickey Mouse. He never **will grow** old!

You know that verbs that tell about actions happening now are in the present tense. Which verbs show present tense?

Some verbs show actions that have gone by. They are in the past tense. Which verbs are in the past tense?

Look at the paragraph again. Which verb is in the future tense?

PRACTICE/APPLY

A. (Written) Write the verbs.

Example: 1. lived

(1) Long ago, only Native Americans lived in America. (2) Then other people came. (3) They traveled on ships. (4) Now we hear tales of these people. (5) We know about the Pilgrims. (6) At the show, you will learn about them.

(7) You will see all the Pilgrims' homes. **(8)** People there speak like Pilgrims. **(9)** They dress like them, too. **(10)** They will tell you about the Pilgrims.

B. (Written) Rewrite this paragraph. Use the correct tense for each verb.

My mother (live) in Canada when she was little. She (play) hockey after school. Today she (live) in the United States. Next summer she (visit) her mother in Canada.

Putting Steps in Order

How do you give good directions? What does a person need to know? Think about what is done in each step. Then put the steps in order.

Tell why these directions are not clear.

Boiling an Egg (Incorrect)

Take the shell off the egg.

Cook the egg for 15 minutes.

Put the egg in a pan of water.

Bring the water to a boil.

The directions are not in order. If you do what they say, you will not have a hard-boiled egg. You will have boiled egg shells! The directions make sense when the order is fixed.

Boiling an Egg (Correct)

1. Put the egg in a pan of water.

2. Bring the water to a boil.

3. Cook the egg for 15 minutes.

4. Take the shell off the egg.

PRACTICE

A. **(Oral)** These directions are not in order. Tell them in the right order.

Washing Dishes (Incorrect)

Let the clean dishes dry.

Scrape any food off the dishes.

Then wash them in soapy water.

B. **(Written)** These directions are not in order. Write the steps in order.

Packing a Lunch (Incorrect)

Put the paper bag in a cooler.

Wrap it in waxed paper.

Put it and your drink in a paper bag.

Make your sandwich.

APPLY

Think of something you can do with an egg. Write two sentences about it. Put the steps in order.

Giving Directions

You often give directions. You may tell a friend how to get to your home. You may tell how to play a game.

Giving good directions takes thought. What does someone need to know? You must think about each step. If you do not, you may leave out something important.

Read these directions.

Making an Emergency Call (Incorrect)

Dial "O" and wait for the operator to answer.
Tell your name, address, and phone number.
Do not hang up until told to do so.

One step is missing. Do you know what it is? It is that the operator must be told the problem.

Making an Emergency Call (Correct)

1. Dial "O" and wait for the operator to answer.
2. Tell the operator what the problem is.
3. Tell your name, address, and phone number.
4. Do not hang up until told to do so.

These directions make sense. The missing step has been added.

PRACTICE

A. (Oral) Read the list of topics. Choose one that you like to do. Decide how to tell someone how to do it. Put the steps in order. Be ready to give your directions aloud.

drawing a rainbow   drawing a square

making a sock puppet   making a card

making a bookmark   drawing a face

B. (Written) These directions are not in order. Also, one step is missing. Decide what step is missing. Then write all the steps in order.

Making a Peanut Butter and Banana Sandwich

Spread peanut butter on one slice of bread.

Put the two pieces of bread together.

Get out the bread, peanut butter, and banana.

APPLY

Think about sweeping the floor. How do you do it? Write two sentences telling how you sweep the floor. Put the steps in order.

Using *Am, Is,* and *Are*

> **Use *am* with *I*. Use *is* with other singular subjects. Use *are* with plural subjects.**
>
> I|<u>am</u> here. She|<u>is</u> there. They|<u>are</u> going.

Use the verb *is* with singular subjects. Singular subjects mean *he, she,* or *it.*

Read these sentences.

> Jon **is** happy. He **is** glad. **Is** Pam here?

The subject of the first sentence is *Jon.* *Jon* means the same thing as *he.* The verb *is* is used. What are the subjects in the next two sentences? What verbs are used?

Use *are* with plural subjects. Plural subjects mean *we* or *they.* Use *are* with the word *you.*

Look how *are* is used here.

> They **are** friends. You **are** right.

What are the subjects? What are the verbs?

The word *I* is special. It is the only subject that goes with the verb *am.*

Use the Word Bank. It will help you to remember when to use *am, is,* and *are.*

WORD BANK

Singular

I am
you are
he is
she is
it is

Plural

we are
you are
they are

PRACTICE

A. (Oral) Tell the correct verb for each sentence.

> **Example:** We (is/are) learning about signs.
> **are**

1. Pam (is/are) talking with her hands.
2. (Is/Are) she using sign language?
3. Her friend (is/are) using it.
4. They (is/are) talking to each other.
5. I (is/am) interested in the signs.
6. You (is/are) able to speak without words.
7. Many people (is/are) using hand signs.
8. An umpire (is/are) always giving signs.

B. (Written) Write each sentence. Use *am, is,* or *are.*

> **Example:** He _____ waving to me.
> **is**

1. _____ you looking at pictures?
2. A picture _____ one kind of talking.
3. Pictures _____ often used to say something.
4. A big shoe _____ hanging outside the store.
5. _____ this store a shoe store?
6. A red light _____ saying "stop."
7. I _____ often talking without words.

APPLY

Think of some signs you have seen. Write three sentences about them. Use *am, is,* and *are.*

Matching Subjects and Verbs

> **Subjects and verbs must match.**
> **Singular:** The cat | purrs.
> **Plural:** The kittens | purr, too.

Sentence subjects and verbs must match. Use the *s*-form of the verb with a subject that means *he, she,* or *it.*

Look at these examples.

The road | **is** busy.   The girl | **walks** safely.

What is the subject of the first sentence? Use *is* with a subject that means *it.* The subject of the next sentence is *The girl.* Use the *s*-form of the verb *walk.*

Do not use the *s*-form with plural subjects that mean *we, you,* or *they.* Do not use the *s*-form if the subject is *I.*

Name the subject and verb in each sentence.

The cars move slowly.
You walk to school.
The streets without sidewalks are wide.
Dogs bark.
Cats meow.
A bird sings.

PRACTICE

A. (Oral) Tell the correct verb for each sentence.

    Example: They (<u>is/are</u>) riding safely.
             are

1. Rob (<u>ride/rides</u>) his bike.
2. The friends (<u>ride/rides</u>) together.
3. The cars (<u>travel/travels</u>) in the right lane.
4. Erin (<u>is/are</u>) looking at traffic signs.
5. People on bikes (<u>stop/stops</u>) at red lights.
6. Erin (<u>is/are</u>) riding her bike.
7. She (<u>is/are</u>) riding behind Rob.

B. (Written) Write the subject and verb in each sentence. Draw a line under singular subjects.

    Example: The girls walk at the same time.
          The girls walk

1. Lisa is behind Karen.
2. They are on the sidewalk.
3. The cars drive toward them.
4. The driver of the red car sees them.
5. He waves at the girls.
6. Lisa waves back at her dad.
7. They stop at the corner.

APPLY

    Suppose you are teaching a first-grader to cross the street safely. Write two sentences telling what you will do.

Irregular Verbs

> **Do not add -ed to form the past tense of an irregular verb.**
>
> Jan, throw the ball. Wow, you <u>threw</u> it too fast!

Verbs in the past tense tell about a time that has gone by. It is easy to form the past tense of most verbs. You add *-ed*.

Look at these verbs.

Regular Verbs

Present	Past
jump	jumped
look	looked

Some verbs are called *irregular verbs*. You must change these verbs to form the past tense.

Notice how these verbs change in the past tense.

Irregular Verbs

Present	Past	Present	Past
know	knew	teach	taught
throw	threw	catch	caught

PRACTICE

A. (Oral) Tell the correct verb for each sentence.

> **Example:** Last year Juan (teaches/taught) his dog to sit.
> **taught**

1. Now Jim (catches/caught) the ball easily.
2. Last week he (catches/caught) it poorly.
3. Last Saturday Alice (teaches/taught) him some tricks.
4. Before this Jim (knows/knew) to watch the ball.
5. Now he (knows/knew) when to grab it.
6. Now Alice (threw/throws) better, too.

B. (Written) Write the verb in each sentence. Underline the verbs in the past tense.

> **Example:** Gail caught the ball.
> **caught**

1. I catch the red bus.
2. Mom taught me the directions.
3. I know the bus driver.
4. We threw the money in the coin box.
5. Art throws a quarter.
6. I caught it falling out.
7. We all know the way now.

APPLY

Write one sentence using the past tense of *know* or *teach*. Then write one sentence using the past tense of *throw* or *catch*.

Review the Basics II

A. Using *Am, Is,* and *Are*

Write each sentence. Use *am, is,* or *are.* (*pages 114–115*)

1. ____ your last name Smith?
2. That ____ a common name here.
3. Other names ____ common, too.
4. ____ you named Chang?
5. Chang ____ a common Chinese name.
6. I ____ Ana Perez.
7. Many people in Spain ____ named Perez.
8. Names ____ interesting.

B. Matching Subjects and Verbs

Write the correct verb for each sentence. (*pages 116–117*)

1. Many plants (is/are) beautiful.
2. A buttercup (grow/grows) in our yard.
3. One mushroom in the yard (is/are) purple.
4. Dad (plant/plants) flower seeds.
5. These plants (look/looks) pretty.
6. They (is/are) not good to eat, though.
7. The people in my family (enjoy/enjoys) plants.
8. I (watch/watches) my baby sister carefully.
9. She (is/are) too little to understand.
10. Many babies (taste/tastes) everything.

C. Irregular Verbs

Write the correct verb for each sentence. *(pages 118–119)*

1. Yesterday my dentist (teaches/taught) me something.
2. Now she (teaches/taught) it to everyone.
3. Now I (know/knew) how to clean my teeth.
4. I (know/knew) how to brush before.
5. Yesterday she (teaches/taught) me to brush each tooth.
6. Now you (teach/taught) others.
7. Last year my parents (know/knew) another dentist.
8. They (know/knew) I like this one now.

D. More Irregular Verbs

Write the correct verb for each sentence. *(pages 118–119)*

1. Last year the pitcher (throws/threw) fast balls.
2. Now he (throws/threw) curves.
3. Yesterday Bonnie (catches/caught) one.
4. Then she (throws/threw) it back to him.
5. Last week Otto (catches/caught) for us.
6. He (catches/caught) now at practice.
7. Now Otto (throws/threw) fast balls.
8. Otto and Bonnie (catch/caught) better now.
9. Now the pitcher (throws/threw) better, too.
10. He even (throws/threw) well last year.

Business Letters

One day you may write a letter to a business. This kind of letter is a *business letter*. Like an invitation, it answers WH-questions. Do you remember what you learned in Unit 1 about WH-questions? They ask *who, what,* and *when.* They may ask *where, why,* or *how.* Remember that an invitation has five parts. A business letter has the same parts. It also has an *inside address.*

Study this letter.

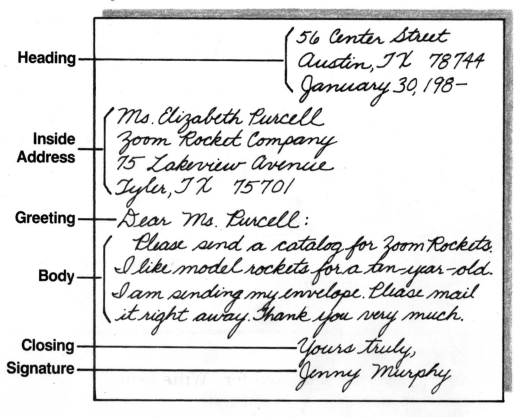

Heading — 56 Center Street
Austin, TX 78744
January 30, 198—

Inside Address — Ms. Elizabeth Purcell
Zoom Rocket Company
75 Lakeview Avenue
Tyler, TX 75701

Greeting — Dear Ms. Purcell:

Body — Please send a catalog for Zoom Rockets. I like model rockets for a ten-year-old. I am sending my envelope. Please mail it right away. Thank you very much.

Closing — Yours truly,

Signature — Jenny Murphy

PRACTICE

A. (Oral) What is the name of each letter part?

1. Dear Mr. Supremo:

2. 908 Eliot Street
Delta, UT 84624
July 18, 198—

3. Yours truly,

4. Mrs. Frances Lang
46 Green Street
Ashland, MI 17450

B. (Written) Write the letter parts in order.

Dear Mr. Blake:

Yours truly,
Daryl Rivers

Mr. Robert Blake
Sunny Juice Company
Miami, FL 33142
111 Lemon Lane

3 Devon Lane
Bridgeport, CT 06611
March 5, 198—

Please send me one copy of your book. It is called "Start a Juice Stand." Enclosed are two labels from Sunny Juice.

APPLY

Think of something to send for. Write two sentences about it.

A Business Letter:
Plan, Write, Edit

You have learned that a business letter is a special letter. You must tell all the facts. The person who gets the letter must know what you want.

Study this letter.

Heading — 72 Ridley Road
Malden, MA 02148
September 5, 198—

Inside Address — Ms. Karen Cole
Screamers Fan Club
Box 666
Long Beach, CA 90806

Greeting — Dear Ms. Cole:

Body — I am a fan of the Screamers Band. I would like to have a picture of the Screamers. I would also like to be a member of the Screamers Fan Club. I have enclosed 50 cents for my dues. Please send the picture soon. Thank you.

Closing — Yours truly,
Signature — William Brody

PLAN

Plan your own letter now. Choose a topic. You might send for a yo-yo that glows in the dark. You might enter your dog's picture in the Cute Puppy Contest. Make notes on what you will write.

You know that a business letter has six parts. It has a *heading* and an *inside address.* It has a *greeting* and *body.* You end with the *closing* and *signature.* The letter answers WH-questions. It may tell *who, what, where, when, why,* or *how.* All the facts needed should be given.

WRITE

Begin with the heading. Write the whole letter. Use the sample on page 124 for the correct form.

Read your letter for the WH-questions. Tell whom the letter is from. Tell what you want. Tell where to send the item or information. You may need to tell how to send it. How will you pay for it? Tell when you want it.

EDIT

When you finish, fix any mistakes. Practice on this letter. There is something missing in the heading. You will need to add two capital letters and a comma. A fact needs to be added. Check the signature. Write this letter correctly.

San Diego, CA 92132
April 14, 198—

mrs. Zelda Walsh
National Park Service
Washington, D.C. 20240

Dear Mrs. Walsh:

my family will visit two parks. We need to know about camps. Could you please send facts?

Yours truly
Jeffrey

Use the Guidelines to fix your letter.

GUIDELINES

1. Answer WH-questions.
2. Include the six letter parts.
3. Capitalize correctly.
4. Check all punctuation marks.
5. Use verb tenses correctly.

Remember to edit carefully. Make your letter correct. Then copy it in your best handwriting.

Envelope Addresses

You address an envelope in a special way. Then the mail carriers know where to take it. Study this envelope.

Sender's Address —

Receiver's Address —

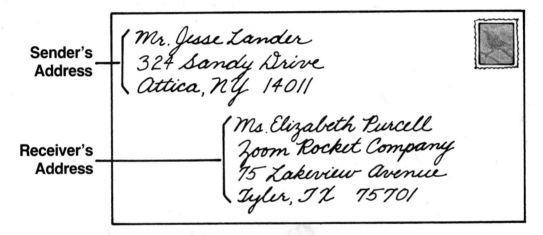

Put the *sender's address* at the top left. Center the *receiver's address*. Each address part goes on a new line. Remember to use ZIP Codes.

PRACTICE

(Written) Draw an envelope. Address it. Use the names and addresses in the letter on page 124.

APPLY

Write two sentences. Tell who you would like to have write to you. Tell why.

Making Introductions

What do you do when you meet someone you do not know? You introduce yourself. You tell your name. You ask the other person his or her name. Sometimes you know two people who do not know each other. Then you introduce them. When you introduce two people, say both names clearly. Try to tell something about each one.

Jill and Susan are walking down the street. Jill sees her classmate Bobby. Jill will introduce Susan and Bobby.

Read Jill's introduction.

Jill: Hi, Bobby! This is my friend Susan. She is from my old neighborhood. Bobby is in my class.

Bobby: Hi, Susan! I remember hearing about you.

Susan: Hi! Do you like your school as much as Jill does?

PRACTICE/APPLY

A. (Oral) Find two partners. Have one person introduce the other two. Follow the Guidelines. Take turns making the introductions.

B. (Oral) Have one person pretend to be Mr. Buzz. Have the second person be Mrs. Grick. Here are some facts about them.

Mr. Buzz collects butterflies. He just came back from a trip to Fripland. He found many butterflies. Mrs. Grick used to live in Fripland.

Introduce the two people. Follow the Guidelines.

Unit 3 Test

A. Verb Tenses
Write the present tense of each verb. *(pages 100–101)*

1. Many people (visit) Mount Saint Helens.
2. Hot rock (come) from this mountain.
3. It (spill) thick dust.
4. A scientist (watch) the volcano carefully.

Write the past tense of each verb. *(pages 102–103)*

5. People (watch) a volcano grow in Mexico.
6. A farmer (discover) it.
7. The farmer (plow) his field.
8. He (notice) smoke.

Write the future tense of each verb. *(pages 104–105)*

9. You (learn) of many volcanoes.
10. You (see) them in books.
11. Volcanoes (form) in some mountains.
12. Only a few (smoke).

B. Using *Am, Is,* and *Are*
Write the correct verb. *(pages 114–115)*

1. I (are/am) learning about train whistles.
2. They (are/am) pleasant to hear.

3. Some whistles (<u>are</u>/is) sending messages.

4. The short whistle (are/<u>is</u>) saying "stop."

C. Matching Subjects and Verbs
Write the correct verb. *(pages 116–117)*

1. The girls (<u>look</u>/looks) at the book.

2. The pictures (is/<u>are</u>) beautiful.

3. Two plants in the pictures (<u>seem</u>/seems) real.

D. Irregular Verbs
Write the correct verb. *(pages 118–119)*

1. Now Doris (<u>teaches</u>/taught) the crafts class.

2. Last week we (know/<u>knew</u>) what to do.

3. Yesterday I (throw/<u>threw</u>) the trash away.

4. Look at Betsy (catch/<u>caught</u>) the ball!

E. Writing
You want to join the Hopscotch Club. Write a business letter. Use your address and today's date for the heading. Put the letter parts below in the right place. Write the body. *(pages 124–126)*

Inside Address   Mr. Joel Torres
　　　　　　　　　Hopscotch Club
　　　　　　　　　P.O. Box 89
　　　　　　　　　Denver, CO 33701

Greeting Dear Mr. Torres: **Closing** Sincerely yours,

Keep Practicing

A. Nouns
Write the nouns in each sentence. *(Unit 2, Lesson 1)*

1. Many people use knots.
2. Sailors tie up their boats.
3. People tie bundles of paper.
4. Divers are tied to a rope.
5. People who fish tie their hooks.
6. A net is made of knotted string.
7. There are many uses for knots.
8. A doctor makes tiny knots.
9. Do your shoes have knots?
10. Some knots have wonderful names.
11. Lace is made from small knots.
12. A bow has a knot, too.
13. There is a bird that is called a knot.
14. The word has different meanings.

B. Plural Nouns
Write the plural form of each noun. *(Unit 2, Lessons 2, 3)*

1. zipper	7. card	13. class	19. box
2. family	8. willow	14. fox	20. tooth
3. noise	9. dish	15. smile	21. penny
4. chest	10. scratch	16. woman	22. branch
5. city	11. hour	17. food	23. teacher
6. crown	12. evening	18. wish	24. bunch

C. Proper Nouns

Find each proper noun. Write it correctly. *(Unit 2, Lessons 4, 5)*

1. esther howland should be famous.
2. You use her idea each february.
3. She lived in worcester.
4. That is a big city in massachusetts.
5. esther made millions of cards.
6. They were for valentine's day.
7. I like this holiday to fall on a monday.
8. This year the holiday is on saturday.
9. Everyone at washington school makes cards.
10. We drop them in the elm street mailbox.

D. Using *A, An,* and *The*

Write the correct article. *(Unit 2, Lesson 10)*

1. Have you seen (a/an) rainbow?
2. You may see one after (a/an) rain.
3. The sun shines through (an/the) clouds.
4. There are many colors in (a/an) rainbow.
5. John saw (a/an) big one yesterday.
6. It went across (an/the) whole sky.
7. I have seen (a/an) rainbow, too.
8. It was (a/an) unusual sight.
9. I saw (a/an) airplane, too.
10. It flew across (an/the) rainbow.
11. That was (a/an) odd thing.

E. Possessive Nouns

Show possession using fewer words. Write possessive nouns. *(Unit 2, Lessons 11, 12)*

1. the drummer of the band
2. the sticks that the drummer owns
3. the songs of the singers
4. the feet of the marchers
5. the costumes of the actor
6. the desk of the teacher
7. the truck the man has
8. the cheers of the crowd
9. the score the team has
10. the wheat the farmer has
11. the horses of the ranchers
12. the calf the cow has

F. Using Commas

Write each sentence correctly. Put commas where they belong. *(Unit 2, Lesson 8)*

1. Andrew's birthday is July 2 1976.
2. He likes hiking reading and skating.
3. Mary John and Tim are his best friends.
4. They all went to the parade on July 4 1983.
5. They liked the fireworks flags and music.
6. In the parade were the marchers drummers and horses.
7. They will all go to the fair on August 30 1984.

8. They all want to see the lambs pigs and rabbits.
9. There will be contests games and rides.
10. I went to the fair on July 29 1982.

G. Capitals and Commas in Letters
Write each letter part correctly. *(Unit 2, Lesson 9)*

1. 14 Elm street
   chicago Illinois 60611
   april 15 198—

2. 12 first street
   Houston Texas 77001
   July 8 198—

3. 301 george Street
   Denver colorado 80201
   June 9 198—

4. Dear Art
   your friend
   Mary

5. Dear Lin
   sincerely
   Janet

6. Dear ana
   your friend
   tony

H. Abbreviations
Write the abbreviations for these words. *(Unit 2, Lesson 7)*

1. Sunday
2. October
3. December
4. February
5. August
6. Wednesday
7. Doctor
8. Friday
9. January

Write the abbreviations for the underlined words.

10. Third Street
11. Lake Road
12. Arizona
13. Park Avenue
14. Elm Street
15. California
16. Winter Road
17. Texas
18. Channing Road

Something Extra

In the News

Glenna Davies is a reporter. She wrote a story for her school newspaper. The story is about a bicycle parade that will take place in her town. Read the news story on page 137. Look for the facts.

Who will be in the parade?
What kind of parade is it?
When will the parade be?
Where will it take place?

Glenna answered all these questions in her story. Reporters always give the most important facts in the first few sentences of their stories. They answer the questions *who, what, when,* and *where.*

Write Away!

Pretend you are a reporter for your school newspaper. Write a short news story about a school event. Get the most important facts. *Whom* is the story about? *What* is happening? *When* and *where* is it happening? Write all these facts in the first paragraph. Here are some ideas to get you started.

singing teacher catches cold
students put on funny play
school runs out of pencils and paper

NICKEL NEWS

Bloomtown School
Bicycle Parade Is Back!

Many children from Bloomtown School will take part in the Bicycle Parade. It will be at City Park next Friday at 4 o'clock.

On Monday Mr. Brooks will start taking names of people who want to be in the parade. All bikes must be inspected by 5 P.M. on Thursday.

Prizes will be given for the funniest and prettiest bicycle in each grade. A grand prize ribbon will be given for the most unusual bike.

Last year Alice Cramer won the grand prize ribbon. Alice hopes to win again this year!

—*Glenna Davies*

Halfway Down

Halfway down the stairs
Is a stair
Where I sit.
There isn't any
Other stair
Quite like
It.
I'm not at the bottom,
I'm not at the top;
So this is the stair
Where
I always
Stop.

Halfway up the stairs
Isn't up,
And isn't down.
It isn't in the nursery,
It isn't in the town.
And all sorts of funny thoughts
Run round my head:
"It isn't really
Anywhere!
It's somewhere else
Instead"

—*A. A. Milne*

4

Describing
Places

SKILLS TO BUILD ON

Adjectives and Adverbs
The Dictionary
Synonyms and Antonyms
Prefixes

PRACTICAL APPLICATIONS

Writing a Description
Talking about a Scene

Adjectives

> An *adjective* is a word that tells about a noun.
> It may tell color, size, or shape.
>
> <u>red</u> apples <u>big</u> apple <u>round</u> apple

You know that a noun names a person, place, or thing. An *adjective* tells about a noun. It adds detail. An adjective may tell the color or size of something. It may tell the shape.

Look at these sentences.

> The fox hunts animals.
> The **blue** fox hunts **small** animals.

Notice the adjectives in the second sentence. They tell about the nouns. The word *fox* is a noun. The word *blue* is an adjective. It tells about the fox. It tells the color of the fox. The adjective *small* tells about the noun *animals*.

Find the adjectives in these sentences.

> A blue fox has thick fur.
> Its ears are round and short.
> It has a bushy tail.

Which nouns do they tell about?

Adjectives make your writing interesting.

PRACTICE

A. (Oral) Find the adjective in each sentence. Say what it is.

> **Example:** The hungry fox eats insects.
> **hungry**

1. The red fox eats fruit.
2. The fox has a long tail.
3. The tail has a white tip.
4. The clever fox lives in a den.
5. The den might be a hollow log.
6. It may be in sandy soil.
7. The fox likes a safe den.

B. (Written) Tell more about each noun. Write an adjective for each one.

> **Example:** field
> **green field**

1. eyes
2. winter
3. hair
4. snow
5. berry
6. nose
7. teeth
8. sky
9. forest
10. box
11. frog
12. table

APPLY

Think of an animal. Write two sentences about its home. Use an adjective in each sentence.

Adjectives for the Senses

> **Adjectives** can tell how things look, sound, smell, taste, or feel.
>
> <u>Look</u>: dusty road   <u>Sound</u>: loud bark   <u>Smell</u>: fresh air
> <u>Taste</u>: salty soup   <u>Feel</u>: cold wind

An *adjective* tells more about a noun. An adjective can describe what your senses tell you.

Seeing and hearing are two of your senses. Adjectives can tell how things look or sound.

Look at these adjectives.

> The **shiny** apple fell. Clyde gave a **loud** cry.

These adjectives tell about what you see or hear. Your senses pick up these details.

Look at these groups of words.

> the cat's **soft** fur   the **sour** pickle

Which adjective tells how something feels? Which tells about taste? Look at the chart.

Adjectives

Sight	Sound	Touch	Smell	Taste
bright	loud	bumpy	fresh	sour
red	quiet	hard	sweet	salty

PRACTICE

A. (Oral) Each sentence has an adjective that tells about one sense. Tell what that adjective is.

> **Example:** The clock has a loud alarm.
> **loud**

1. Lynn bought a purple plum at the stand.
2. We keep crunchy celery in a jar.
3. Ken likes the sweet smell of roses.
4. My foot hit the sharp edge of the table.
5. The loud horn made Norma jump.
6. The dog buried a juicy bone.

B. (Written) Complete each sentence. Write an adjective. It should tell about the sense that is given. Use words from the chart if you need help.

> **Example:** Her shoes are _(sight)_.
> **shiny**

1. The _(hearing)_ telephone woke us.
2. Harry stared at the _(sight)_ light.
3. That _(touch)_ sweater is mine.
4. We picked some _(smell)_ flowers.
5. We cooked a _(taste)_ stew.
6. We all laughed at my _(sight)_ hat.

APPLY

Suppose you are in an empty house. What is it like? Write two sentences about it. Use your senses. Draw a line under the adjectives.

Using Adjectives That Compare

> **An adjective can be changed to show how one thing compares with another thing or things.**
>
> The milk is <u>cold</u>.   Iced water is <u>colder</u>.
> Ice cubes are <u>coldest</u>.

When you compare two things, use the ending *-er*. Also use the word *than*. When you compare three or more things, use the ending *-est*.

Study the rules in the chart. What adjective compares two things? What adjective compares three or more things?

Forming Adjectives That Compare

To make many adjectives mean "more" or "most," add *-er* or *-est*.	short shorter shortest
Some adjectives end with a consonant letter and *y*. Change the *y* to *i* and add *-er* or *-est*.	tiny tinier tiniest
Some adjectives end with a final *e*. Drop the *e* and add *-er* or *-est*.	nice nicer nicest
Some adjectives end with a single vowel and a single final consonant letter. Double the final consonant and add *-er* or *-est*.	wet wetter wettest

PRACTICE

A. (Oral) Tell the correct adjective for each sentence.

Example: A bat is (<u>smaller</u>/smallest) than a crow.
smaller

Large

1. The brown bat is the (faster/<u>fastest</u>) of all bats.
2. It is (<u>smaller</u>/smallest) than the red bat.
3. Its body is (<u>furrier</u>/furriest) than its wings.
4. A scared bat is the (noisier/<u>noisiest</u>) of any bat.
5. Its hearing is (<u>sharper</u>/sharpest) than its sight.
6. The (older/<u>oldest</u>) bats of all live more than twenty years.

Larger

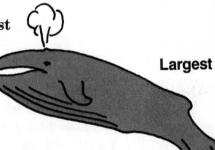

B. (Written) Copy the headings below. Write each adjective. Then add *-er* and *-est* to each.

Example: cold

Adjective	-er	-est
cold	colder	coldest

Largest

Headings

Adjective	-er	-est

1. pale
2. pretty
3. old
4. hot
5. large
6. cozy

APPLY

What are some differences between a kitten and a lion? Write two sentences that compare them. Use an adjective in each sentence.

Using *More* and *Most* with Adjectives

> **To compare one thing with another thing or things, use *more* or *most* with some adjectives.**
>
> interesting   more interesting   most interesting

Adjectives help compare things. To compare, you change some adjectives. You can add *-er* or *-est*.

Some adjectives make comparisons another way. You do not add endings. You use *more* and *most*.

Look at these examples.

> Mike is **more helpful** than Sal.
> The **most wonderful** show is in town!

How do these sentences compare things? They use *more* to compare two things. They use *most* to compare three or more things.

Adjectives that use *more* and *most* are alike in one way.

How are these adjectives alike?

> beautiful   delicious   terrific

How many syllables does each word have? Do not add *-er* or *-est* to long adjectives. Use *more* and *most*.

PRACTICE

A. (Oral) Find the mistakes in the sentences.
Read the corrected sentences aloud.

> **Example:** This shirt is most colorful than that one.
> **This shirt is more colorful than that one.**

1. Rob is most likable than Angela.
2. The more colorful coat of all the coats was red.
3. Their plan is most organized than ours.
4. I bought the more lovable of the three hamsters.
5. He is the more generous person I know.
6. This window is most open than that one.

B. (Written) Complete each sentence with *more* or
most.

> **Example:** Of the three books, this is the ____ exciting.
> **most**

1. My note was the ____ mysterious of all.
2. Josh is the ____ cheerful boy in our class.
3. Yen Yen is ____ careful than Carl.
4. Your picture is ____ colorful than mine.
5. Kathy's dog is a ____ eager eater than Robin's.
6. Sid wore the ____ horrible mask of them all.

APPLY

Suppose you are watching three clowns. One is
curious. One is lovable. One is frightening. Write
three sentences comparing them. Use *more* or
most.

Review the Basics I

A. Adjectives

Write the adjective in each sentence. *(pages 140–141)*

1. Bodies need good food.
2. Pat eats a big breakfast.
3. He needs extra energy.
4. Pat drinks a tall glass of juice.
5. He makes a big bowl of oatmeal.
6. Then he pours on fresh milk.
7. Next he takes a slice of pink ham.
8. He also eats warm rolls.

B. Adjectives for the Senses

Complete each sentence. Write an adjective. It should tell about the sense that is given. *(pages 142–143)*

1. What a __(taste)__ lunch I had!
2. First we ate __(taste)__ hamburgers.
3. These were served on __(touch)__ rolls.
4. I had some __(sight)__ cheese on mine.
5. Mom served __(hearing)__ carrot sticks.
6. We also had __(sight)__ corn.
7. I loved the __(smell)__ campfire.
8. Dad gave us __(taste)__ berries for dessert.

C. Using Adjectives That Compare
Write the correct adjective. *(pages 144–145)*

1. This is my (prettier)/prettiest) penny of all.
2. It is the (nicer/nicest) coin I have.
3. The (duller/dullest) one of all is the nickel.
4. It is (thicker/thickest) than the penny.
5. A dime is (smaller/smallest) than a nickel.
6. It is (thinner/thinnest) than a nickel.
7. A quarter is (bigger/biggest) than a dime.
8. It is the (larger/largest) coin I have.
9. My dollar bill is (new/newer) than yours.
10. This dime is the (older/oldest) one I have.

D. Using *More* and *Most* with Adjectives
Complete each sentence with *more* or *most*.
(pages 146–147)

1. My cat is ____ patient than my dog.
2. Of my three aunts, Aunt Em is the ____ generous.
3. Your story is ____ surprising than mine.
4. We give Granddad the ____ comfortable chair of all.
5. The house is on the ____ beautiful road in town.
6. Yesterday, Al was ____ cheerful than Benjamin.
7. That cat is the ____ beautiful one here.
8. Today is ____ pleasant than Monday.

Adjectives in a Paragraph

Adjectives tell about nouns. They may tell about color, size, or shape. They may tell about sight or sound. They may tell how something feels, smells, or tastes.

You have also seen that adjectives help to compare things. You can add *-er* or *-est* to some adjectives. Use the words *more* or *most* with others.

Find the adjectives in this paragraph.

Our country has wonderful roads. Shaggy brown animals helped make them. Huge herds of buffalo used to live here. Their feet wore deep paths. People traveled the dusty trails. Sometimes they were the safest routes. Old paths are still used. New roads cover them now.

Did you find nine adjectives?

PRACTICE/APPLY

A. (Written) Read the paragraph. Write all the adjectives you find.

Example: 1. interesting

(1) The sloth is an interesting animal. (2) It is also a slow animal. (3) You can find faster snails! (4) Sloths live in warm places. (5) They have long toes. (6) You need good eyes to see the shy animals. (7) Some even have green fur. (8) Small plants give them the odd color.

B. (Written) Read the next paragraph. Think of adjectives to complete the sentences. Write the adjectives.

Example: 9. large

Some animals have __(9)__ bodies. Others have __(10)__ ones. Some have __(11)__ fur. Others have __(12)__ scales. Many animals live in __(13)__ forests. Some like __(14)__ weather. Libraries have __(15)__ books about animals.

The Dictionary

A *dictionary* tells about words. These words are called *entry words*. The entry words are listed in a dictionary in alphabetical order.

Each page has *guide words* to help you. The guide words are at the top of each page. The guide words tell you the first and last entry words on the page.

Look at the sample.

---

fill | fingerprint   219

fill (fil), **1** make full; put into until there is room for nothing more: *Fill this bottle with water. We filled the pots with soil.* **2** become full: *The well filled with water.* **3** take up all the space in; spread throughout: *The crowd filled the hall. Smoke filled the room.* **4** stop up or close by putting something in: *The dentist filled my tooth.* **5** hold and do the duties of (a position or office): *We need someone to fill the office of president. verb.*

fi nal ly (fī′nl ē), **1** at the end; at last: *The lost dog finally came home.* **2** in such a way as to decide or settle the question: *They must tackle the issue finally. adverb.*

fi nance (fə nans′ or fī′nans), **1** money matters: *A successful banker must have skill in finance.* **2** **finances,** money matters; funds; revenues: *New taxes were needed to increase the nation's finances. noun.*

Only part of the page is showing. Can you tell what the last entry word is?

To find words quickly, think of the dictionary in three parts. Look for words that begin with *A-F* in or near the first part. Words that start with *G-P* will be in the middle. Words that start with *Q-Z* will be in the last part.

PRACTICE

A. (Oral) Look at the different meanings of the word *fill*. Decide which meaning of *fill* fits each sentence. Read aloud the meaning for each sentence.

> **Example:** We filled the glass
> with milk.
> **make full**

1. The dentist will <u>fill</u> my tooth.
2. The team <u>filled</u> the bus.
3. <u>Fill</u> the bucket with water.
4. He will <u>fill</u> the hole with dirt.
5. She will <u>fill</u> the role of leader.

B. (Written) Write these sets of guide words on your paper.

daisy|dust   jam|jewel   jib|just

Now write each entry word under the right set of guide words.

Example: daisy|dust
dream

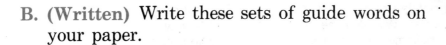

dream   jell   deal   joke   jaw   jingle
jet   dig   jolly   dog   jar   join

APPLY

Write two sentences using different meanings of the word *fill*.

Words with the Same Meaning

Words that have almost the same meaning are *synonyms*.

Look at the synonyms in these sentences.

The shrew is small.
The shrew is little.

Small and *little* are synonyms. There is a way to remember what synonyms are. *Synonym* starts with *s*. So does the word *same*. *Synonyms* mean "almost the same."

PRACTICE

(Written) Write each word in List A. Then write a synonym for each one from List B.

Example: start
        start—begin

List A		**List B**	
1. frighten	4. scream	present	happy
2. big	5. gift	scare	mad
3. angry	6. cheerful	large	yell

APPLY

Write two sentences using synonyms.

Words with Different Meanings

Some words have meanings that are almost opposite. These words are *antonyms*.

Look at the antonyms in these sentences.

Shrews are found in **wet** and **dry** places.
Their tails can be **long** or **short**.

Wet and *dry* are antonyms. *Wet* is the opposite of *dry*. What antonyms are in the second sentence?

PRACTICE

(Written) Read each pair of words. If they have an opposite meaning, write *A* for *antonym*. There are eleven antonyms.

Example: up/down
   A

1. hard/soft
2. high/low
3. crooked/bent
4. stop/go
5. thick/thin

6. happy/glad
7. inside/outside
8. pull/push
9. slow/quick
10. tall/short

11. light/dark
12. big/huge
13. empty/full
14. big/large
15. end/begin

APPLY

Write two sentences. Use two antonyms.

Prefixes

You can make new words by putting word parts together. A *prefix* is a word part. It is added to the beginning of a word. It changes the word's meaning. When you add a prefix to a root word, you make a new word.

Prefixes have their own meanings. Each one changes root words. One useful prefix is *un-*. It means "not" or "do the opposite of."

Look at these examples.

Root Words   **Prefix Added**
happy   unhappy
tie   untie

How is the meaning of each word changed?

Study three more prefixes in the chart.

Prefixes

Prefix	Meaning	Example
re-	again, back	rebuild, replace
in-	inside, in, into, not	inactive
mis-	wrongly, incorrectly	misplace

A word may look like it has a prefix when it does not have one. Check if there is a root word.

Which three of these words have prefixes?

real refill inner inside misspell mist

PRACTICE

A. (Oral) Put each prefix with at least two root words. Make eight new words. Say them.

Prefixes   **Root Words**
 un-   form   correct
 re-   complete tie
 mis-   place   take
 in-   treat   make
        wrap   do

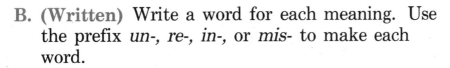

B. (Written) Write a word for each meaning. Use the prefix *un-, re-, in-,* or *mis-* to make each word.

Example: view again
          review

1. not real
2. fill again
3. not correct
4. do the opposite of lock

5. understand incorrectly
6. place back
7. copy again
8. use wrongly

APPLY

Write two sentences about something you do in school. Use a root word in one sentence. Use the same word with a prefix in the next sentence.

10 MORE BASIC SKILLS

Adverbs That Tell Where

> **An *adverb* may tell about a verb. An adverb may answer the question *where*.**
>
> The frightened dog ran <u>away</u>.

Some words tell about other words. You know that adjectives tell about nouns. *Adverbs* tell about other kinds of words. They may tell more about verbs. Some adverbs tell where things happen.

Read this sentence.

The frog jumped **up.**

Where did the frog jump? It jumped up. The word *up* is used as an adverb. It tells *where*. It tells about the verb *jumped.*

Now look at these sentences.

Alex searched **<u>everywhere.</u>**
The frog jumped **away.**

Which words are adverbs? They answer the question *where*. Which words do they tell about?

The Word Bank shows some adverbs you may see often. They tell where things happen.

Study the Word Bank.

WORD BANK

here
far
nearby
above
there
near
away
below
up
outside
in
down
inside
out

PRACTICE

A. (Oral) Find the adverb in each sentence that answers the question *where.* Name it.

> **Example:** We will go inside before it rains.
> **inside**

1. Squirrels live everywhere.
2. They do stay outside.
3. A nest is built nearby.
4. The baby squirrels stay inside.
5. We go there to see them.
6. Look up to see the nest.
7. It is hanging above.

B. (Written) Complete each sentence. Write an adverb. It should answer the question *where.*

> **Example:** My dog sleeps ——— in a doghouse.
> **outside**

1. He eats his meals ——— .
2. One puppy is jumping ——— .
3. We played ——— .
4. We are going ——— this summer.
5. Alex is moving ——— .
6. Come ——— !

APPLY

Suppose you have lost something. Write two sentences telling where you might look for it. Use adverbs that tell *where.*

11 MORE BASIC SKILLS

Adverbs That Tell When

> **An adverb may answer the question *when*.**
> Jan will meet them <u>later</u>.

You know that adverbs may answer the question *where*. Adverbs may also tell *when*.

Look at this sentence.

Marco gave a report **yesterday.**

The word *yesterday* is used as an adverb. It tells *when*. It tells about the verb *gave*.

Now look at these sentences.

She fixed the bike **today.**
She painted it **next.**

WORD BANK

next
later
tomorrow
now
lately
first
soon
today
then
early
sometime
yesterday

Which words are adverbs? They answer the question *when*. Which words do they tell about?

Look at the word *soon* in these sentences.

The bus will leave **soon.**
Soon the bus will leave.

An adverb may be put in different places in a sentence. The meaning does not change.

Study the adverbs in the Word Bank.

PRACTICE

A. (Oral) Find the adverb in each sentence that answers the question *when*. Name it.

> **Example:** It is raining now.
> **now**

1. First Sarah got the key.
2. Then she unlocked the door.
3. She went to the kitchen next.
4. The family would eat dinner later.
5. Soon Sarah was looking for a snack.
6. She had seen an apple yesterday.
7. Today she saw a pear.
8. The pear was soon gone.

B. (Written) Complete each sentence. Write an adverb. It should answer the question *when*.

> **Example:** I lost my tooth _____ .
> **yesterday**

1. The game should be finished _____ .
2. I woke up _____ .
3. _____ we will catch the bus.
4. It rained _____ .
5. Luis called me _____ .
6. _____ we will go outside.

APPLY

Plan a picnic. Write two sentences telling what you will do. Use adverbs from the Word Bank.

Adverbs That Tell How

> **An adverb may answer the question _how_.**
> The ponies ran <u>quickly</u>.

You have learned many things about adverbs. You know that they may tell about verbs. They may answer the questions _where_ and _when_. You know that they can be used in different places in a sentence. The sentence meaning will not change.

There is one more thing about adverbs for you to know. Adverbs may answer the question _how_.

Look at this sentence.

Sue sang **softly**.

WORD BANK

bravely
softly
carefully
sadly
neatly
wisely
clearly
loudly
happily
quickly
proudly
patiently

The word _softly_ is used as an adverb. It tells _how_. It tells about the verb _sang_.

Look at the adverbs here.

Charles drank his milk **slowly.**
The kittens slept **quietly.**

Which words are adverbs? They answer the question _how_. Which words do they tell about?

Study the adverbs in the Word Bank.

They answer the question _how_. Many adverbs tell how. Most of them end in -_ly_.

PRACTICE

A. (Oral) Find the adverb in each sentence that answers the question *how.* Name it.

> **Example:** Jan wrote her name carefully.
> **carefully**

1. Charles spelled every word correctly.
2. We looked into the box carefully.
3. It is raining steadily.
4. They walked slowly.
5. He beat the eggs briskly.
6. The door opened suddenly.
7. We joyfully greeted our cousin.
8. The fire burned brightly.

B. (Written) Complete each sentence. Write an adverb. It should answer the question *how.*

> **Example:** Les ran to the store _____ .
> **quickly**

1. He explained the directions _____ .
2. The coach shouted _____ .
3. The dog barked _____ .
4. We folded the wash _____ .
5. _____ we marched to the music.
6. The stars were shining _____ .

APPLY

Can you thread a needle? Write two sentences about it. Use an adverb that tells *how* in each one.

13 MORE BASIC SKILLS

Forming Adverbs

> **Many *adverbs* end in *-ly*. Some adjectives can be changed to adverbs by adding *-ly.***
>
> adjective   adverb
> It is a slow boat. The boat moved slowly.

You know that adverbs may tell about verbs. You have studied adverbs that tell how something is done. An action may be done slowly, for example. It may be done carefully.

These adverbs end with *-ly*. The *-ly* ending can be added to many adjectives. This changes the adjectives into adverbs.

Read these examples.

> Chris is a **quiet** boy. He works **quietly.**
>
> Alan is a **loud** boy. He talks **loudly.**

The words *quiet* and *loud* are adjectives. Each tells more about a noun. When the ending *-ly* is added, the word changes. It becomes an adverb. It tells about a verb. The adverb *quietly* tells about the verb *works*. What verb does *loudly* tell about?

Look at the Word Bank.

Each word in the first list is an adjective. The word becomes an adverb when *-ly* is added.

WORD BANK

Adjective

soft
sweet
careful
quick

Adverb

softly
sweetly
carefully
quickly

Every word that ends in *-ly* is not an adverb.
Some adjectives end this way.

PRACTICE

A. **(Oral)** Look at the underlined word in each
sentence. Tell if the word is an adjective or an
adverb.

Example: It was done <u>properly</u>.
adverb

1. Bonnie <u>gladly</u> proved her point.
2. She filled the cup with <u>chilly</u> water.
3. She <u>quickly</u> froze it.
4. One <u>silly</u> person giggled.
5. Bonnie <u>proudly</u> showed the ice to us.
6. She <u>carefully</u> showed us how big it was.
7. Ice <u>clearly</u> took more space than water.

B. **(Written)** Write each word as an adverb.

Example: careful
carefully

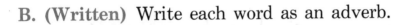

1. bright	3. eager	5. fair	7. bold
2. neat	4. bad	6. playful	8. close

APPLY

Write two sentences about a ball game or ball
players. Use an adjective from Practice B. Then
change it to an adverb. Use the adverb.

Review the Basics II

A. Adverbs That Tell Where
Find the adverb in each sentence that answers the question *where*. Write it. *(pages 158–159)*

1. We looked everywhere for the basket.
2. We could not find it anywhere.
3. Did you look here?
4. I looked there.
5. Lisa went outside.
6. She looked up.
7. Rain was coming down.
8. She could not see the sun anywhere.
9. Lisa ran inside.

B. Adverbs That Tell When
Find the adverb in each sentence that answers the question *when*. Write it. *(pages 160–161)*

1. The Masons camp often.
2. They will go soon.
3. Today Lisa thinks of something.
4. Now she remembers the first-aid kit.
5. She does not forget it often.
6. First she goes to the chest.
7. Then Lisa finds what she needs.
8. Next she checks it all.

C. Adverbs That Tell How
Find the adverb in each sentence that answers the question *how*. Write it. *(pages 162–163)*

1. They happily plan their trip.
2. The Masons pack the box quickly.
3. Lisa wraps the tape carefully.
4. She tightly seals the box.
5. They wisely take a first-aid kit.
6. The car is packed neatly.
7. Lisa quietly falls asleep.
8. They arrive safely.
9. The Masons eagerly unpack.
10. The campfire burns brightly.

D. Forming Adverbs
Write each word as an adverb. *(pages 164–165)*

1. smooth
2. slow
3. loose
4. light
5. calm
6. sudden
7. sweet
8. careful
9. near
10. quick
11. close
12. sharp
13. neat
14. clean
15. brave
16. bright

Clues for Space Order

Do you live near or far from your school? Words like *near* and *far* help you tell about space order. They help describe where something is. Some space-order words are shown in the Word Bank. Each word could help you tell where something is.

Now study the picture.

It is a picture of a city park. Suppose someone asked you to tell about the picture. What would you say? Answer the questions on page 169. They will help you to describe the picture.

Is the pond at the **top** or **bottom?**

Are the skyscrapers **near** or **far?**

Where are the old brick buildings? Are they **in front of** or **behind** the skyscrapers?

Where are the joggers? Are they on the **left** side or the **right** side of the pond?

Is the woman with her dog **next to** or **across from** the bench?

Are the ducks **inside** or **outside** of the fence?

Answer all the questions when you tell about the picture. Then you will tell where everything is.

PRACTICE

A. **(Oral)** Look at the picture. With your classmates, tell what things are *near.* Then tell what things are *far away.*

B. **(Written)** Study the same picture. Now list the things that are in the *left* part of the picture. List the things that are in the *right* part of the picture.

APPLY

Write two sentences that tell where your desk is in your classroom. Use three words from the Word Bank.

15 COMMUNICATING

Details

When you tell about something, you describe it. One way to describe something is to give details.

What if someone named Mary said she had a dog. Would you know anything about it? What if she said, "I have a big, brown dog. It has long, soft fur. It has a very loud bark." Now you know about the dog. Mary told you details.

Which senses did Mary use?

Think about the words Mary used to describe her dog. She used adjectives. She used her senses to give *details.*

When you tell someone about something, try to use details. Use adjectives that describe. Think about the five senses. They are *sight, sound, touch, smell,* and *taste.* Remember them when you want to describe something.

What sense might be used for each detail?

red	loud	humming	hot	musty
fuzzy	tiny	bumpy	sour	rough
smoky	sweet	screeching	old	wet

PRACTICE

A. (Oral) Study the picture. Pretend you are one of the people in it. Try to describe everything around you.

Make a list of the details you will describe. Tell them. Use the questions to help you.

What do you see?   What do you taste?
What do you hear?   What do you feel?
What do you smell?

Think about being in different parts of the picture.

B. **(Written)** If you could be somewhere else, where would you be? Think about a scene that is not your classroom. Write a list of details that describe the place. Use your senses to help with the details.

APPLY

Think of a special breakfast. Write two sentences describing it.

A Description: Plan, Write, Edit

A *description* is a word picture. It pictures something for the reader. Adjectives help describe. Words that tell about space order also help describe.

PLAN

Look at the picture of the circus. Think what you would tell a friend about the circus. What would you see? What would you smell? What would you hear? What would you taste and feel? Take notes. List three to five words to answer each question.

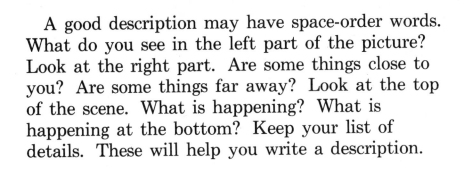

A good description may have space-order words. What do you see in the left part of the picture? Look at the right part. Are some things close to you? Are some things far away? Look at the top of the scene. What is happening? What is happening at the bottom? Keep your list of details. These will help you write a description.

WRITE

Think of the circus as a picture. Begin with the left side. What is happening there? Are you sitting near the top or bottom of the picture?

Write your description. Include clear details. Include adjectives to describe nouns. Think of what you would sense. Use space-order words like *left, right, near, far, top,* and *bottom.* Describe the scene so that someone who has never seen it can imagine it.

EDIT

Practice editing on this description. Write it. Fix the four mistakes.

Use the Guidelines for help.

Last week, I went to a three-ring circus. Ten clowns were in the ring on the left. They squeezed into a car. Their act was good. In the middle ring were the acrobats. They were up so high! They almost touched the bottom of the room. The last rings was far away. I couldn't see it. Even so, I did hear the lions roar loudly. They were the excitingest part of the circus.

Now edit your own description.

GUIDELINES

1. Use adjectives that describe what your senses tell you.
2. Use words that describe space.
3. Use adjectives and adverbs correctly.

Is your description complete? Pretend that you have never seen the picture of the circus. Now read the description to yourself. Would you be able to picture it now?

After you edit your description, copy it in your best handwriting.

Talking about a Scene

A good way to describe is to tell details you might sense. Pretend you spent the day at a zoo.

Think about these questions.

What can I see?	What can I feel?
What can I taste?	What can I smell?
What can I hear?	

Now tell a friend about it. Act out what you would say. It is started for you. Make up details. Your friend should ask questions about the senses.

You: I had such a great time at the zoo! I wish you had gone with me!

Your friend: Well, tell me all about it.

You: I saw funny brown monkeys and tall giraffes. My favorite animal was the lion.

Your friend: What noise did the lion make?

PRACTICE/APPLY

(Oral) Act out this talk with a partner. Your partner should think of more questions to ask.

You: On Saturday, I climbed to the top of Mount Crag.

Your partner: What did you see at the top? How did your legs feel after the climb?

Unit 4 Test

A. Adjectives
Write the adjective in each sentence. *(pages 140–143)*

1. Bones guard important parts of the body.
2. They also help make new blood.
3. Our arms and legs have long bones.
4. Soft material is in the middle of a bone.
5. It is covered by a hard shell.
6. A bad break in a bone will mend.
7. Ana broke a small bone in her foot.
8. She has a white cast on it.

B. Using Adjectives That Compare
Write the correct adjective for each sentence. *(pages 144–147)*

1. Spaghetti is (<u>thinner/thinnest</u>) than noodles.
2. Your ring is (<u>smaller/smallest</u>) than mine.
3. My snack was (<u>deliciouser/more delicious</u>) than Kay's.
4. That bird is the (<u>noisier/noisiest</u>) in the flock.
5. I just saw the (<u>more/most</u>) awful show of all!
6. Nana is (<u>older/oldest</u>) than Bart.
7. That is the (<u>fuzzier/fuzziest</u>) hat I have ever seen.
8. Jeff's skates are (<u>newer/newest</u>) than Amy's.

C. Adverbs That Tell Where
Find the adverb that answers the question *where* in each sentence. Write it. *(pages 158–159)*

1. Miners may dig underground for coal.
2. One miner looks up.
3. He sees coal everywhere.
4. More miners work nearby.

D. Adverbs That Tell When
Find the adverb that answers the question *when* in each sentence. Write it. *(pages 160–161)*

1. Now miners hold lights.
2. Sometimes rocks can fall.
3. Coal is often shipped.
4. Finally the coal arrives!

E. Adverbs That Tell How
Find the adverb that answers the question *how* in each sentence. Write it. *(pages 162–163)*

1. Miners work hard at their jobs.
2. They watch carefully for danger.
3. Coal can burn steadily.

F. Writing
Look at the picture on page 168. Write a description of the park. Use space order. Use adjectives for detail. *(pages 172–174)*

Keep Practicing

A. Verbs
Write the verb in each sentence. *(Unit 3, Lessons 1 and 2)*

1. My friend Lai Ling has an odd pet.
2. Her pet is an unusual plant.
3. We watched the Venus's-flytrap.
4. It ate a bug right before our eyes!
5. Sometimes flies smell this plant.
6. Then they touch its leaves.
7. The leaves trap the bug!
8. Now the leaves open.
9. I will buy my own plant.
10. I will give it a name.

B. Present Tense
Write the correct present tense verb for each sentence. *(Unit 3, Lesson 3)*

1. Helen (watch/watches) a movie about small animals.
2. Suddenly, the parrot (ask/asks) for a cracker.
3. The scouts (pick/picks) up roadside litter.
4. Every night, Fiona (wish/wishes) on the first star.
5. Abby and Carl always (miss/misses) the early bus.
6. My sisters (try/tries) to keep their room neat.
7. I (want/wants) to play that game.
8. You (pick/picks) the corn.

C. Past Tense

Write the verbs that are in the past tense. *(Unit 3, Lesson 4)*

1. Ted (hands/handed) Donna the magnets.
2. One magnet (picked/picks) up paper clips.
3. Then Donna (drops/dropped) some pins.
4. She (pushed/pushes) the magnet toward a pin.
5. Slowly, the pin (moved/moves), too.
6. Some pins even (jumps/jumped) in the air.
7. Next Donna (touches/touched) one pin to another.
8. The magnet (lifts/lifted) both pins up in the air.
9. Then Ted (tried/tries) picking up paper.
10. He (cries/cried), "The magnet only lifts steel!"

D. Future Tense

Write the verbs that are in the future tense. *(Unit 3, Lesson 5)*

1. Some day I will fly in a rocket.
2. Water covers much of the earth.
3. The sun shines in the daytime.
4. The sun will shine on the earth.
5. The sun will warm the soil and water.
6. The earth will turn.
7. Then the sun shines on the other side.
8. The earth will move around the sun.

E. Using *Am, Is,* and *Are*

Write the correct verb for each sentence. *(Unit 3, Lesson 9)*

1. The sun (is/are) millions of miles away.
2. It (are/is) a yellow star.
3. The planets (is/are) around it.
4. Earth (is/are) warmed by the sun.
5. Many people (is/are) using its energy.
6. The moon (are/is) closer to the earth.
7. You (is/are) looking at it.
8. I (is/am) looking also.
9. People (is/are) able to reach the moon.
10. Moon rocks (is/are) in our museum.
11. I (is/am) reading about them.
12. The book (is/are) interesting.

F. Irregular Verbs

Write the correct verb for each sentence. *(Unit 3, Lesson 11)*

1. Last year I (catches/caught) chicken pox.
2. Yesterday Al (taught/teaches) his dog to sit.
3. Now watch me (throw/threw) this ball.
4. We (knew/know) that song last year.
5. Now they (taught/teach) little babies how to swim.

6. Now Liz (catches/caught) every ball we throw to her.

7. Dad said people (throw/threw) rice at his wedding.

8. Now I (knew/know) all the rules for playing soccer.

9. Last week Sue (catches/caught) two fish.

G. Envelope Addresses

Draw the shape of an envelope on your paper. Address it correctly. Use this information. (Unit 3, Lesson 14)

Sender   Chicago, IL 60622
Bill Keith
17 Rice Road

Receiver   67 Irving Place
New York, NY 10003
Children's Book Council

H. Putting Steps in Order

These directions are not in order. Write the directions. Be sure to put the steps in order. *(Unit 3, Lesson 7)*

Move that pot to a sunny spot.
Leave it in the water until it sprouts.
Then plant it in a pot of dirt.
First put the seed in a dish of water.

Something Extra

Alike and Different

Both dogs in the picture are walking with their owners. In some ways, both dogs are alike. Each is large and black. Each has curly hair.

The dogs are different in an important way. Sue is walking a well-trained dog. It walks quietly next to its owner. The other dog seems to be walking Jim. It is barking. It does not seem to be trained at all.

Pretend that the picture was not shown on page 182. You probably could read the words and then draw the picture.

In a way, the writer drew a picture with words. The writer told what ways the dogs were alike. The writer told how they were different, too.

Write Away!

Look at the picture on this page. Choose two of the dogs. Write a few sentences. Tell how the dogs are alike and how they are different. Think about their size and color. What kind of hair do they have? How are they acting? Here are some words to help you.

both	different from	listens	noisy
larger	not trained	spotted	sitting
each one	at attention	neither	wagging

Bedtime

Five minutes, five minutes more, please!
    Let me stay five minutes more!
Can't I just finish the castle
    I'm building here on the floor?
Can't I just finish the story
    I'm reading here in my book?
Can't I just finish this bead-chain—
    It *almost* is finished, look!
Can't I just finish this game, please?
    When a game's once begun
It's a pity never to find out
    Whether you've lost or won.
Can't I just stay five minutes?
    Well, can't I stay just four?
Three minutes, then? two minutes?
    Can't I stay *one* minute more?

—*Eleanor Farjeon*

5

Being
Persuasive

SKILLS TO BUILD ON

Pronouns
Contractions with Pronouns
Fact and Opinion
Words That Persuade

PRACTICAL APPLICATIONS

Writing an Argument
Giving a Speech

Pronouns

A *pronoun* stands for one or more nouns. If it takes the place of a noun in the subject, it is called a *subject pronoun.*

Josh | walks the dog and the goat.
<u>He</u> | walks the dog and the goat.

A noun is often the subject of a sentence. A *pronoun* can be the subject, too.

Look at the pronouns in these sentences.

Dad reads the paper. **He** reads the paper.
The weather report is on the last page. **It** is on the last page.

The pronoun *he* stands for *Dad. He* is the subject of the sentence. What pronoun is the subject of the last sentence? What noun does it stand for?

A pronoun can stand for more than one noun.

Look at this example.

Mom and Dad share the paper. **They** read a section at a time.

What two nouns does the pronoun *they* stand for?

More subject pronouns are shown in the Word Bank. Use each pronoun in a sentence.

WORD BANK

Subject Pronouns
I
you
he
she
it
we
they

PRACTICE

A. (Oral) Tell which pronoun is correct.

> **Example:** (She/Her) gave the book to Ana.
> **She**

1. At eight o'clock (they/them) woke up.
2. (It/He) is Saturday morning.
3. (Us/We) watch a show about baby seals.
4. (It/She) is in color.
5. After lunch, (we/us) go to the library.
6. (I/Us) find a nature magazine.
7. (He/Him) wrote a story about baby seals.

B. (Written) Find the subject of each sentence. Decide which pronoun should stand for it. Write the pronoun.

> **Example:** Bill likes television.
> **He**

1. Grandma tells stories about old television shows.
2. Mistakes used to appear on the screen.
3. Sometimes an actor would trip over a cable.
4. Perhaps an actress would forget a speech.
5. Mother and Dad have a big wooden television.
6. Today the stations show many taped programs.

APPLY

Think of a cartoon character. Using a noun as the subject, write one sentence about the character. Then write two sentences using subject pronouns.

More Pronouns

> **Some pronouns are used as the subjects of sentences. Other pronouns are used in other parts of sentences.**
>
> My sister|saw Ruth. My sister|saw <u>her</u>.

You know that a subject pronoun may take the place of a subject noun. What about nouns that are not the subject? Nouns are used in other parts of a sentence, too. Other pronouns take the place of these nouns.

Look at these examples.

Our class is reading about gold. We like to read about **it.**

My aunt is taking Lee and Jack to the museum. She is taking **them** to see the pictures.

The pronoun *it* takes the place of *gold.* The pronoun *them* takes the place of two nouns. What nouns does *them* replace?

Read the pronouns in the Word Bank.

The pronouns *you* and *it* may be used as the subject. They may also be used in other parts of the sentence. The other pronouns in the Word Bank are not used as subjects.

WORD BANK

Pronouns in Other Sentence Parts

me
you
him
her
it
us
them

PRACTICE

A. (Oral) Tell which pronoun is correct.

> **Example:** We went with (they/<u>them</u>) to the museum.
> **them**

1. In 1922 Howard Carter found (they/<u>it</u>).
2. King Tut's tomb was discovered by (<u>him</u>/he).
3. Miss Hayes showed pictures of the tomb to (<u>us</u>/we).
4. We enjoyed seeing (<u>them</u>/they).

B. (Written) Read each sentence. Decide which pronoun can take the place of the underlined word or words. Write the pronoun.

> **Example:** Grandma called <u>Ruth</u>.
> **her**

1. Grandma told <u>Ruth and Ted</u> some stories about horses.
2. One story was about a horse that raced <u>a train</u>.
3. Another story was about horses that pulled <u>trains</u>.
4. They thanked <u>Grandma</u> for telling the stories.
5. They told <u>Jack</u> about the stories.

APPLY

Suppose you found a bag of coins. What would you do? Write three sentences. In each sentence use a pronoun that is not a subject pronoun.

Using *I* or *Me*

> ***I* is a subject pronoun. *Me* is used in other parts of a sentence.**
>
> I|like summer.   Ken|visits <u>me</u>.

You use the pronouns *I* and *me* when you talk about yourself. Use *I* only as a subject pronoun. You know that the subject tells who does, is, or has something. Use the pronoun *me* in other parts of a sentence.

Look how *I* and *me* are used below.

> **I** use many ice cubes.
> Ms. Sorel told **me** some stories about ice.

What is the subject of each sentence?

When you talk about yourself and someone else, name yourself last.

Study these examples.

> Ms. Sorel and **I** saw people cutting ice.
> They looked funny to Ms. Sorel and **me**.

What is the subject in each sentence? Why is the pronoun *me* used in the second sentence? Whose name appears first both times?

PRACTICE

A. (Oral) Tell which pronoun should complete each sentence.

> **Example:** Anna told Victor and (I/me) about collecting bottles.
> **me**

1. Last week Victor and (I/me) went hunting.
2. He and (I/me) went digging for old bottles.
3. Anna took Victor and (I/me) to the spot.
4. Victor and (I/me) took shovels.
5. In an hour, Victor and (I/me) had found nine bottles.
6. Victor and (I/me) liked the blue one best.

B. (Written) Read each sentence. Write the pronoun *I* or *me* to complete each one.

> **Example:** Today ＿＿＿ learned about ice.
> **I**

1. Today someone might hand ＿＿＿ an ice cube.
2. In 1850 they might have taken ＿＿＿ outside.
3. ＿＿＿ would have to go to the ice house.
4. ＿＿＿ would see ice inside the ice house.
5. Someone would give ＿＿＿ an ice pick.
6. First ＿＿＿ would wipe off the sawdust.
7. People would tell ＿＿＿ to be careful.

APPLY

Suppose you had to use candles for light. How would your life be different? Write three sentences about it. Use *I* in two sentences. Use *me* in one.

Pronouns in Sentences

> **The pronouns *it* and *you* may be used in any part of a sentence.**
>
> *You* came home. The letter is for *you*.

You have learned that subject pronouns stand for one or more nouns in the subject. Other pronouns are used in other parts of a sentence.

If a pronoun is not the subject of a sentence, you know that you will often use a different pronoun. The pronouns *it* and *you* may be used in any part of a sentence.

Look at these examples.

> A teddy bear was mailed to **you.**
> **It** arrived yesterday.
> Soon **you** will put **it** on the bed.

Which sentences have subject pronouns? In what two places is the pronoun *it* used?

Look back at the Word Banks on pages 186 and 188. What two words are the same in both Word Banks?

When you are the subject, use the pronoun *I.* When you talk about yourself and someone else, name yourself last. Use *I* or *me.*

PRACTICE

A. (Oral) Name the pronoun in each sentence. Tell if it is or is not a subject pronoun.

> **Example:** He has a teddy bear.
> **He—subject pronoun**

1. Teddy bears were named for him.
2. He was President Theodore Roosevelt.
3. People called him "Teddy."
4. There was a cartoon of the bear and him.
5. Nell's parents showed the cartoon to her.
6. Maybe you have seen Teddy and the bear.
7. Now I know the story.

B. (Written) Replace the underlined words with pronouns. Write the sentences.

> **Example:** We looked for <u>Susie and Kim</u>.
> **We looked for them.**

1. <u>You and I</u> like to listen to stories.
2. Ellen will tell <u>Clara and me</u> a story.
3. Later I will tell <u>Ellen</u> one.
4. One story I like is about <u>a seal</u>.
5. <u>A boy and a girl</u> rescue the baby seal!
6. Now <u>Ellen</u> is laughing.
7. <u>Our stories</u> have happy endings.

APPLY

Invent a food that could be named after you. Describe it in three sentences.

Review the Basics I

A. Pronouns

Find the subject of each sentence. Decide which pronoun could stand for it. Write the pronoun. *(pages 186–187)*

1. Firefighters go to school.
2. Betsy is a firefighter.
3. Cousin Art is one, too.
4. The school teaches many skills.
5. Of course, the school teaches fire fighting.
6. Betsy and Art learn to use the tools.
7. Today Betsy can run up a tall ladder.
8. Art and I are visiting the station later.
9. Betsy will be there.

B. More Pronouns

Read each sentence. Decide which pronoun is correct. Write the pronoun. *(pages 188–189)*

1. Uncle Joe took (I/me) to the ball game.
2. I like (he/him) a lot.
3. (We/Us) often see games together.
4. On my birthday, Aunt Mary gave (I/me) tickets.
5. I thanked (her/she) for the gift.
6. Uncle Joe got (we/us) a program about the ball players.
7. I saw (they/them).
8. The players waved to (we/us).

C. Using *I* or *Me*

Read each sentence. Write the pronoun *I* or *me* to complete each one. *(pages 190–191)*

1. In California ＿＿ have an uncle who acts.
2. Uncle Ray and ＿＿ are good friends.
3. Once Ray and ＿＿ went to the movie studio.
4. The star of the show waved to ＿＿ .
5. ＿＿ watched Ray put on his make-up.
6. The costume room was fun for ＿＿ .
7. When the cameras started, ＿＿ was quiet.
8. An actress gave ＿＿ her picture.

D. Pronouns in Sentences

Find the pronoun in each sentence. Write it. Label it *Subject* or *Not Subject*. *(pages 192–193)*

1. Now we can open the picnic basket!
2. Mrs. Ruis told me.
3. Ralph thanked her for the suntan cream.
4. Jean opened it.
5. The sand scratched us.
6. Picnics are fun for us.
7. They are better than a party.
8. The family has them each summer.
9. You can come, too!
10. Someone will call you.

Pronouns in a Paragraph

Pronouns can be used in place of nouns.

Find the pronouns in this paragraph.

I love to do science projects. Mom and Dad
help me. They showed me a great one. You
will love it. First, get baking soda and vinegar.
Then mix them together. The fizz will surprise
you. It surprised me.

Which word is the subject of the first sentence?
In the next sentence, the pronoun *me* is not the
subject. It is in a different part of the sentence.
In sentence six, what does the pronoun *them* stand
for? Is *them* a subject pronoun?

The pronoun *you* appears two times. In which
sentence is it a subject pronoun? Remember, *you*
and *it* may be used in any part of a sentence.
Review the kinds of pronouns.

Subject Pronouns: I, you, he, she, it, we,
they
Pronouns in Other Sentence Parts: me,
you, her, him, it, us, them

Remember to name yourself last.

Harry and **I** laughed.
The feather tickled Harry **and me.**

PRACTICE/APPLY

A. (Written) Rewrite the paragraph. Replace the underlined words with pronouns.

People read stories. John likes animal stories. I gave an animal story to John. Mary likes stories about ships. I found a ship story for Mary. The story had many pictures. Mary and John would like to write stories, too!

B. (Written) Write the paragraph. Fill in the blanks with pronouns.

Dr. Watson is my dentist. I see _____ twice a year. _____ cleans my teeth. _____ shows me how to take care of _____ . Dr. Watson gives _____ a new toothbrush each time.

Facts

Facts are true statements about things or ideas. They can be proved in some way. You can prove some facts by using your senses.

Other facts can be proved by using a book. It might be an encyclopedia. Look at these facts.

Elizabeth Blackwell was born in 1821.

She was the first woman doctor in America.

Today both men and women can be doctors.

PRACTICE

(Written) Write the four sentences that are facts.

Example: Austin is the capital of Texas.
Austin is the capital of Texas.

1. Fish live in water.
2. Teeth are hard.
3. Trees are nice.
4. Clyde is too tall.
5. The sun is hot.
6. Shoes can be green.
7. Cats are good pets.
8. People love all dogs.

APPLY

Write one statement that is a fact.

Opinions

Opinions are not the same as facts. An *opinion* is what a person feels or thinks. An opinion cannot be proved. People may have different opinions.

Read this opinion.

Science is the most exciting subject.

How can you tell that this statement is an opinion? Could it be proved?

PRACTICE

(Written) Write the three opinions.

Example: Math is easy.
Math is easy.

1. May is the best month of the year.
2. Reading is taught in school.
3. A week has seven days.
4. Running is fun.
5. Tuesday comes after Monday.
6. A horse is bigger than a cat.
7. Goats are the best pets.

APPLY

What holiday do you like? Write three sentences about it. Write one fact. Write two opinions.

Words That Persuade

Words can show feelings. They can make you feel you like something. Words can be used to persuade you to like something.

Read this list of words.

beautiful	strong	friendly	gentle
clean	cheerful	tender	lively

Would you like a *cheerful* person? How would you feel about *clean* socks?

Words may persuade you not to like someone or something.

Look at this list.

unfriendly	scratchy
noisy	angry
messy	awful
nosy	spoiled
sneaky	dirty

Would you like something *spoiled*? Would you like something *awful*?

Words can be used to show an opinion. Someone might say the day was *warm and pleasant.* Someone else might call it *hot and unpleasant.* Their words show their feelings.

PRACTICE

A. (Oral) Read each word. Tell if the word would persuade you to like something or not.

1. brave	**5.** sweet	**9.** funny
2. merry	**6.** ugly	**10.** careful
3. selfish	**7.** terrible	**11.** cozy
4. good	**8.** nasty	**12.** bossy

B. (Written) Write the word in each sentence that describes something. Draw a line under it if the word makes you like the thing.

> **Example:** The friendly pony ate a carrot.
> **<u>friendly</u>**

1. Alan has a great horse.
2. The horse is handsome.
3. Once people had strong horses.
4. The gentle animals carried riders.
5. They pulled loads over bumpy roads.
6. At first cars were smelly.
7. The first cars were noisy, too.
8. Drivers now get a smooth ride.

APPLY

Write three sentences about some sneakers. They are orange and green with silver laces. In two sentences, use words that would make someone like the shoes. In the third sentence, make someone dislike them.

Contractions with Pronouns

> A *contraction* is a short way of writing two words.
>
> she + is = <u>she's</u>   we + will = <u>we'll</u>

You can make *contractions* with pronouns and verbs. The contractions are a short way of writing the pronouns and verbs. A letter or letters are dropped. An *apostrophe* (') is used instead.

See how three contractions are written.

Two Words	Contractions
I am	I'm
you will	you'll
they would	they'd

What happens if you forget the apostrophe? What words are formed without the apostrophe? The meaning changes if the apostrophe is left out.

she will→shell, she'll

Look at these examples.

Contractions with *Be* and *Have*

Be		Have
I am→I'm they are→they're		you have→you've
he is→he's you are→you're		it has→it's
it is→it's they are→they're		he had→he'd

PRACTICE

A. (Oral) Name the contractions.

> **Example:** She'll meet us there.
> **She'll**

1. At noon I've got to leave.
2. Carmen, you'll know the time.
3. You see, she's wearing a watch.
4. Now he's telling time.
5. You're wearing watches with faces.
6. You can see that they're easy to read.
7. I'm looking at the short hand.

B. (Written) Decide how to change each pronoun and verb to a contraction. Write the sentences using the contractions.

> **Example:** I am early today.
> **I'm early today.**

1. They would enjoy swimming at the lake.
2. He has found a duckling.
3. Now she will find four eggs.
4. You have walked far.
5. Shhh, you are waking the baby!
6. If my sisters were here, they would laugh.
7. It is not supposed to buzz.

APPLY

Imagine the teacher has brought a huge box into class. Write three sentences telling what might be inside. Use contractions in each sentence.

Too Many Nouns

> **Two sentences may repeat a noun. It may be better to use a pronoun in the second one.**
>
> It
> The boat was unloaded. ~~The boat~~ was ready to sail.

You have learned that pronouns may take the place of nouns. A subject pronoun takes the place of a noun that is the subject. Other pronouns take the place of nouns that are not subjects.

You can replace a subject noun that is repeated. Replace it with a subject pronoun. What subject noun is repeated here?

> **Pirates** really sailed.
> **Pirates** sailed to many places.

What pronoun replaced the noun?

> **Pirates** really sailed.
> **They** sailed to many places.

Pronouns can replace repeated nouns in other sentence parts, too.

Look at these sentences.

> John found the **maps.**
> He read the **maps** carefully.

What pronoun could replace *maps?*

PRACTICE

A. (Written) Read each pair of sentences. Rewrite the second sentence. Use a subject pronoun in place of the repeated word or words.

Example: Blackbeard was a pirate. <u>Blackbeard</u> was English.
He was English.

1. This pirate lived over 250 years ago. <u>This pirate</u> was famous.
2. People say he had gold. <u>People</u> think it is still buried.
3. Liza and I saw a map. <u>Liza and I</u> copied it.
4. The map is old. <u>The map</u> shows an island.

B. (Written) Read each pair of sentences. Rewrite the second sentence. Use the correct pronoun in place of the repeated word or words.

Example: In 1938 we had a radio. We liked <u>a radio</u>.
We liked it.

5. The family listened to the shows. I loved <u>the shows</u>.
6. I sat next to Mom. Dad sat next to <u>Mom</u>, too.
7. One show scared people. It really frightened <u>people</u>.
8. People heard the play. They thought <u>the play</u> was true.

APPLY

Write two sentences about treasure. Use a subject pronoun in one. In the other sentence, use a pronoun that is not the subject.

Too Many Pronouns

> **When you use a subject pronoun, be sure to drop the subject noun or nouns.**
>
> <u>Incorrect</u>: The car it is new.
> <u>Correct</u>: The car is new. <u>Or</u>: It is new.

You know that a pronoun takes the place of a noun or nouns. A subject pronoun replaces a subject noun. Use *either* the noun or the pronoun. Do not use both of them in one sentence.

Look at these sentences.

> **Sandy** is my cousin. **Sandy she** took a trip.

What is wrong with the second sentence? The pronoun *she* should replace *Sandy*. Both words should not be used in the subject. *Sandy* and *she* mean the same person. Only one of the words is needed.

A subject pronoun can replace more than one noun. You still follow the same rule. Use *either* the pronoun or the nouns.

Look at these sentences.

> **Uncle Steve, Sandy, and I** went by car.
> **Uncle Steve, Sandy, and I we** had fun.

How would you fix the second sentence?

PRACTICE

A. (Oral) In six sentences, pronouns should be dropped. Some have subject nouns and pronouns that mean the same thing. Read the sentences aloud. Tell which pronouns to drop.

Example: Stamps they are fun to collect.
they

1. Sandy and I we kept a scrapbook.
2. A scrapbook it is fun to make.
3. You need some blank pages.
4. Each day Sandy she saved little things.
5. Once Uncle Steve he bought oranges for us.
6. The oranges they were juicy.
7. The clerk he gave us a fancy bag.
8. Sandy saves things like that.

B. (Written) Read the paragraph. Check the subjects carefully. Make sure there is a capital letter at the beginning of each sentence. Write the paragraph. Correct the five mistakes.

Shooting stars they can be seen in the summer. A friend she told me about shooting stars. She and I we saw one. we picked a clear night. My friend she saw dozens of them. I fell asleep!

APPLY

Write a pair of sentences about shooting stars. Use a subject pronoun in the second sentence.

Review the Basics II

A. Contractions with Pronouns
Write the contraction in each sentence. *(pages 202-203)*

1. I think you've heard of Loch Ness.
2. It's a lake in Scotland.
3. I'm told the lake is deep.
4. Someday I'd like to visit it with my family.
5. We'll try to see the Loch Ness monster.
6. You're thinking that the monster is not real.
7. Maybe I'll take a picture of it.
8. Then you'd know Nessie is real!

Decide how to change each pronoun and verb to a contraction. Write the sentences using the contractions. *(pages 202-203)*

9. You have carried the camera.
10. I have bought the film.
11. Now we will have fun.
12. First you will tell Sonia the joke.
13. Then she will laugh.
14. I will take her picture.
15. She will enjoy having nice ones.
16. They would be a good birthday present.
17. She is happy.

B. Too Many Nouns

Read each pair of sentences. Rewrite the second sentence. Use a pronoun in place of the word or words repeated. *(pages 204–205)*

1. Dottie was crying. <u>Dottie</u> was sad.
2. Tim heard her. <u>Tim</u> was worried.
3. Tim ran to Dottie. He talked to <u>Dottie</u>.
4. Dottie pointed to her feet. She lifted one of <u>her feet</u>.
5. "My feet hurt. <u>My feet</u> are sore!"
6. Tim looked at her feet. He looked at <u>her feet</u> carefully.
7. "I see your feet. Something is wrong with <u>your feet</u>."
8. "Your shoes are wrong. <u>Your shoes</u> are on the wrong feet."
9. Dottie looked at her feet. She turned <u>her feet</u> around.
10. "My feet are not wrong! <u>My feet</u> are the only ones I have!"

C. Too Many Pronouns

In four sentences, pronouns should be dropped. Fix those sentences. *(pages 206–207)*

1. Our class we learned about salt.
2. Some people get it from sea water.
3. Also, salt it comes from mines.
4. Your tears are salty.
5. People they need salt.
6. You and I we need some salt.

12 COMMUNICATING

Reasons

Have you ever wanted to make someone agree with you about something? First you must tell your opinion. Then you should give *reasons* why you have this opinion. Often the word *because* comes before a reason.

Read this sentence.

> We shouldn't ride our bikes **because** it is too dark.

The person thinks that riding bikes is a bad idea. What is the reason? The part of the sentence that comes after *because* tells the reason. It tells why we should not ride our bikes. A reason should always answer the question *why*.

What are the reasons in these sentences?

> I want to go swimming because it is so hot.
> The dog is not happy because a jogger ran past.
> Skating is fun because you go so fast.
> Collecting stamps is good because you learn about places.

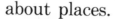

PRACTICE

A. (Oral) Read this list of opinions. Tell a reason for each opinion.

Example: Riding a bike is good because _____.
it builds muscles

1. I like to dance because _____.
2. I wish it would rain today because _____.
3. I wish it would never rain because _____.
4. Mittens are better than gloves because _____.

B. (Written) Read the opinions in **List A.** Then read the reasons in **List B.** Match each opinion with a reason. Write the complete sentence.

Example: Rain is good because it helps things grow.

List A	List B
1. Our team is the best	because you feel the wind.
2. Having a pet is good	because it doesn't eat much.
3. Sailing a boat is fun	because you are never alone.
4. A goldfish is a good pet	because you can make up your own.
5. A story without an ending is good	because we practice a lot.

APPLY

Write three sentences about your favorite season. Write an opinion and at least one reason.

Arguments

Think about times when you want someone to agree with you. You argue for your point of view. This does not mean that you are fighting. It means you are telling someone your *argument*.

Do you want someone to listen to your opinion? You have seen that you must use facts and reasons. Be sure your facts are true.

Read this argument.

I think our school should have a swimming pool because everyone should learn to swim. It is good exercise. If everyone knew how to swim, fewer people would drown.

This a good argument. Find the opinion, the reason, and the facts. The facts are true. Does the reason answer the question *why*? Would this argument persuade you that the school needs a swimming pool?

PRACTICE

A. (Oral) Read the opinion in each argument. Then tell if the argument has good reasons and true facts.

1. I think everyone should have a pet. Pets teach you to be responsible. Pets have to be fed and kept clean.
2. I think everyone should have a hobby. Hobbies help you learn. Hobbies take your mind off your problems.
3. I like oranges better than grapefruits. Oranges are a bright color. You can squeeze them.
4. I think grapes without seeds are better than grapes with seeds. You don't ever swallow a seed by mistake. You don't have to find a place to put the seeds when you are done.

B. (Written) Read this argument. Write the opinion.

I think weekends should be three days long. There would be more time to get things done. We would have more time to visit friends. There would be more time to have fun. People would work or go to school for only four days. They would be better rested after the weekend.

APPLY

Write three sentences. Give your opinion about learning to cook. Be sure to tell reasons and facts.

14 COMMUNICATING

An Argument:
Plan, Write, Edit

To write an argument, you must begin with an opinion. It must be backed up with reasons and facts. Follow these steps to plan, write, and edit an argument. See who can be persuaded to agree with you!

PLAN

What do you think about people sitting on the grass in parks? What is your opinion?

Study the pictures.

Should the people be sitting on the grass?
Should they not sit on the grass?

Read the Guidelines.

The Guidelines tell you how to write an argument. Use them to plan a good one.

WRITE

Write your argument. Use your notes. First write your opinion. Then write reasons and facts for your opinion. Give good reasons. Make sure they answer the question *why.*

EDIT

Practice editing on the following argument. Are the reasons good ones? Check the pronouns. Are the contractions written correctly? Rewrite the paragraph. Correct all the mistakes.

Use the Guidelines for help.

I think that sitting on the grass in the park should not be allowed. People they will crush the grass. I'm afraid that me and you will not be able to see grass. Then well never come to the park.

GUIDELINES

1. Tell your opinion.
2. Give reasons and facts that tell why.
3. Check all contractions.
4. Check all pronouns.

Now edit your own argument. Use the Guidelines if you need help. Then copy your argument in your best handwriting.

15 COMMUNICATING

Telling an Opinion

Sometimes you may talk to many people at the same time. Often notes can help you to remember what you want to say. Look at these notes.

Opinion: Cats make good pets.
Reasons: don't eat much, keep you
company, keep themselves clean
Ending: cats, good pets, mine, best of all

Pretend that your family is planning a vacation. Would you like to go camping? Would you rather go swimming? Prepare a talk.

Study the Guidelines.

GUIDELINES

1. Plan the talk. Decide what your opinion is. Think of your reasons and facts. Think of a good ending.
2. Make notes to help you remember.
3. Look at your notes before you start. Look at the listeners. Speak loudly and clearly.

PRACTICE/APPLY

(Oral) Give your talk to your classmates. Then vote as a class on the best vacation idea.

Unit 5 Test

A. Pronouns
Find the subject of each sentence. Decide which pronoun could stand for it. Write the pronoun. *(pages 186–187)*

1. Mom, Dad, and I live in California.
2. Redwood trees grow here.
3. A redwood tree will grow in Oregon, too.
4. Last year Aunt Bea met a park ranger.
5. The ranger works at the Redwood National Park.

Read each sentence. Decide which pronoun can take the place of the underlined words. Write the pronoun. *(pages 188–189)*

6. At the park we saw <u>tall trees</u>.
7. I saw <u>one big stump</u>.
8. Uncle Dan showed <u>Aunt Bea and me</u> the rings.
9. I told <u>Aunt Bea</u> there were hundreds.
10. I could not count all of <u>the rings</u>.

B. Using *I* or *Me*
Read each sentence. Write the pronoun *I* or *me* to complete each one. *(pages 190–191)*

1. Last night ____ saw a red star.
2. Carlos told ____ the star has a name.
3. Carlos and ____ watched the sky.
4. He showed ____ many colored stars.

C. Contractions with Pronouns

Decide how to change each pronoun and verb to a contraction. Write the sentences using the contractions. *(pages 202–203)*

1. Of course <u>they would</u> laugh at the clown.
2. Now <u>you are</u> a Girl Scout.
3. <u>We will</u> eat two dozen sandwiches or more.
4. <u>They are</u> getting ready for school.
5. <u>I will</u> carry the bag.

D. Too Many Nouns

Read each pair of sentences. Rewrite the second sentence. Use a pronoun in place of the repeated word or words. *(pages 204–205)*

1. Mrs. Oka is my neighbor. <u>Mrs. Oka</u> is nice.
2. Jess and I help Mrs. Oka. We like <u>Mrs. Oka</u>.
3. Jess and I carry bags. <u>Jess and I</u> open doors.
4. Mrs. Oka is in a wheelchair. We push <u>the wheelchair</u>.
5. Mrs. Oka likes Jess and me. She thanks <u>Jess and me</u>.
6. Her cats rub against my leg. <u>Her cats</u> purr.

E. Writing

Write an argument about one of the ideas listed below. Tell your opinion. Give at least two good reasons or facts. *(pages 214–216)*

taking pets to school   having school on Saturday

Keep Practicing

A. Matching Subjects and Verbs
Write the correct verb for each sentence. *(Unit 3, Lesson 10)*

1. Now you (is/are) taller than Sam.
2. Martin (push/pushes) the door with his elbow.
3. All of the babies (cry/cries) at once.
4. Tomorrow we (is/are) buying skates.
5. Only one picture (fall/falls) off the wall.
6. The people in the boat (wave/waves).
7. That peanut (is/are) almost round.
8. Eleven clowns (jump/jumps) over the wall.
9. Ned (carry/carries) an egg in each hand.
10. Every afternoon Anna (call/calls) Katy.

B. Adjectives
Write the adjective in each sentence. *(Unit 4, Lessons 1, 2)*

1. Diamonds are hard stones.
2. Diamonds may be large.
3. Diamonds may be yellow.
4. Some become beautiful rings.
5. Even ugly diamonds are used.
6. They cut hard metals.
7. They smooth rough edges.
8. Diamonds are useful stones.

C. Using Adjectives That Compare
Write the correct adjective for each sentence.
(Unit 4, Lesson 3)

1. My math book is (heavier/heaviest) than my reading book.
2. Ms. Ross has the (quieter/quietest) class in the school.
3. That is the (thinner/thinnest) slice I've ever seen.
4. We will be (later/latest) than I said.
5. This pencil is (sharper/sharpest) than yours.

D. Adverbs That Tell Where
Complete each sentence. Write an adverb. It should answer *where. (Unit 4, Lesson 10)*

1. Lions' cages are _____ .
2. At first, the lion was _____ .
3. Then it went _____ .
4. It looked _____ to see something.
5. The lion saw people _____ .

E. Adverbs That Tell When
Complete each sentence. Write an adverb. It should answer *when. (Unit 4, Lesson 11)*

1. Let's play a game of ball _____ .
2. _____ we must find more players.
3. Elly and Ric can play _____ .

4. Pat played ball _____ .
5. Terry will be coming _____ .
6. _____ the twins can play, too.
7. Is your cousin coming _____ ?
8. Maybe _____ would be a better time to play.

F. Adverbs That Tell How
Complete each sentence. Write an adverb. It should answer *how*. *(Unit 4, Lesson 12)*

1. The young colt stood up _____ .
2. It _____ fell again.
3. _____ it struggled up once more.
4. Its mother watched _____ .
5. The colt looked _____ around.
6. _____ it rushed forward.
7. It _____ headed for the door.
8. Its mother followed _____ .

G. The Dictionary
Write these sets of guide words on your paper. *(Unit 4, Lesson 6)*

bad|better   bide|blink   bottle|burn

Write each entry word under the correct set of guide words.

best	bike	badge	barn
big	bud	blackout	boy

H. Words with the Same Meaning
Write each word in List A. Then write a
synonym for each from List B. *(Unit 4, Lesson 7)*

List A
1. calm   2. smile   3. large   4. laugh   5. presents

List B
grin   peaceful   giggle   gifts   big

I. Words with Different Meanings
Read each pair of words. If they have opposite
meanings, write *A* for *antonym. (Unit 4, Lesson 8)*

1. empty/full   5. happy/pleased   9. quick/fast
2. tall/short   6. small/little   10. high/low
3. glad/cheerful   7. thick/thin   11. strong/weak
4. far/near   8. cry/weep   12. quiet/noisy

J. Prefixes
Write a word for each meaning. Use the prefix
un-, re-, in-, or *mis-. (Unit 4, Lesson 9)*

1. use in the wrong way   7. not correct
2. do the opposite of wrap   8. build again
3. not visible   9. spell wrongly
4. lay in the wrong place   10. not complete
5. do again   11. play again
6. do the opposite of tie   12. not able

Something Extra

A Pro's Prose

Read the story on the next page. Fern is a frog. In the story she has feelings and thoughts as though she were a person. Sometimes a writer gives an animal the feelings and actions of a person. The writer pretends that the animal is like a person.

How is Fern feeling? Why?
What does Fern wish for?

Write Away!

Fern's story is not finished. It needs an ending. How would you end the story? What do you think will happen to Fern? Write an ending for the story. Here are some ideas to help you start.

One foggy day Fern heard a splash. She
looked up and saw . . .

Fern decided to leave the lonely pond. She
put on her backpack and . . .

Fern, the Lonely Frog

It was a beautiful spring day. The sun was shining. The sky was clear and blue. The pond sparkled in the sunlight. It had been a long winter. Everyone was glad to be out and about again. Everyone was glad but Fern.

Fern was unhappy. All the other frogs had moved. They went to bigger and better ponds. She had not missed them in the winter. She was resting in her home deep under the mud. Frogs do not go out in the winter. They are used to being alone then. But now it was the spring, and Fern was lonely.

Fern sat on her lily pad. She looked at herself in the water as she brushed a tear from her cheek. She wished she had a friend.

The Picnic

We brought a rug for sitting on,
Our lunch was in a box.
The sand was warm. We didn't wear
Hats or shoes or socks.

Waves came curling up the beach.
We waded. It was fun.
Our sandwiches were different kinds.
I dropped my jelly one.

—Dorothy Aldis

226

6

Telling Stories

SKILLS TO BUILD ON

Matching Nouns and Verbs
Matching Pronouns and Verbs
Helping Verbs and Irregular Verbs
Writing Conversation
Contractions with *Not*

PRACTICAL APPLICATIONS

Writing a Story
Telling a Story

Matching Subjects and Verbs

> **A subject and its verb must match.**
>
> singular subject   *s*-form of verb
> Mrs. Lugo|writes a note.
>
> plural subject   plain form of verb
> Mr. and Mrs. Lugo|write a note.

A subject and its verb must match. The *s-form* of a verb is used with a subject that means *he, she,* or *it.*

Look at this sentence.

Nancy|saves postcards.

The subject of the sentence is *Nancy,* one person. The subject is singular. The matching verb *saves* is in the *s*-form. It ends with an *s.*

A plural subject and its verb should match. Plural subjects mean *we* or *they.* The matching verbs are not in the *s*-form. Use the *plain form.*

Look at these sentences.

The **postcards|show** buildings.
The **girls|sell** the cards.

What are the subjects? What are the verbs?

Remember to use *is* with subjects that mean *he,*
she, or *it.* Use *are* with subjects that mean *we,*
you, or *they.*

PRACTICE

A. (Oral) Tell the correct verb for each sentence.

> **Example:** Marco (paste/pastes) stamps in a book.
> **pastes**

1. My cousins (press/presses) flowers.
2. Flowers with small centers (is/are) best.
3. My cousins (put/puts) the flowers between papers.
4. Old newspapers (is/are) good.
5. Heavy books (lie/lies) on them for a week.
6. A dried flower in a frame (look/looks) pretty.

B. (Written) Write the subjects and verbs.
Underline any subject that is singular.

> **Example:** Marco saves stamps.
> **Marco saves**

1. My friends collect many different things.
2. Lucia saves postcards of flowers.
3. The flowers are pretty.
4. Eva keeps her cards by state.
5. The children put their cards in boxes.

APPLY

Think of a butterfly. Write three sentences
about it. Underline the subjects and verbs.

Matching Pronouns and Verbs

> **A subject pronoun and its verb must match.**
> **She|keeps** old coins. **They|keep** old coins.

You know to use the *s*-form of the verb with subjects that mean *he, she,* or *it.*

Look at these examples.

> **She|buys** stamps.
> **He|likes** space stamps.

The pronoun *I* is different. The plain verb form is used with *I.* The *s*-form is not used.

> **I|save** stamps.

The pronouns *we, you,* and *they* are plural. The plain form of the verb is used with plural pronouns. The *s*-form of the verb is not used.

Look at these sentences.

> **They|come** from many countries.
> **We|take** old stamps off envelopes.

The pronoun *you* can be singular or plural. It is always used with the plain form of the verb.

> **You|collect** animal stamps.

WORD BANK

Pronouns with *s*-form

she
he
it

Pronouns with Plain Form

I
we
you
they

PRACTICE

A. (Oral) Tell the correct verb for each sentence.

> **Example:** We (collect/collects) stamps.
> **collect**

1. Now he (save/saves) stamps.
2. I (soak/soaks) envelopes in water.
3. They (dry/dries) on the kitchen counter.
4. You (press/presses) the stamps flat.
5. At lunch we (trade/trades) extra stamps.
6. She (visit/visits) a stamp store.
7. It (sell/sells) some stamps for a penny.
8. Of course, you (see/sees) rare stamps, too.
9. They (cost/costs) hundreds of dollars each.

B. (Written) Look at each underlined verb. Write its correct form. Some verbs may be correct. Use the *s*-form or the plain form.

> **Example:** He <u>show</u> us his ships.
> **shows**

1. On Saturdays we <u>makes</u> models of ships.
2. We <u>buy</u> paint in tubes.
3. She <u>glue</u> the wood carefully.
4. In a minute, you <u>tries</u> it.
5. It <u>look</u> just like a big ship!

APPLY

Write three sentences. Tell about building something. Use a pronoun in each sentence.

Using *Has* and *Have*

> **Has** and *have* are important verbs.
> She|has the paint. They|have the paint.

If the subject means the same thing as *he, she,* or *it,* use *has.* If the subject means the same thing as *I, you, we,* or *they,* use *have.*

Look at these examples.

He|has a violin. **They|have** drums.

PRACTICE

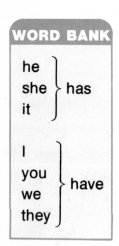

WORD BANK

he
she } has
it

I
you
we } have
they

(Written) Write *has* or *have* for each sentence.

Example: Carlos (have/has) a plan.
         has

1. I (has/have) a picture.
2. We (has/have) crayons.
3. Artists (has/have) ideas for paintings.
4. Ivette (has/have) a piece of paper.
5. She (have/has) an idea for a picture.
6. It (have/has) water and boats in it.

APPLY

Write a sentence using *has* and one using *have.*

Helping Verbs

> A *helping verb* goes with a *main verb*. *Have* and *has* may be used as helping verbs.
>
> helping verb   main verb
> The girls have found the crayons.

In the first sentence, *has* is a helping verb. What is the main verb in the second sentence?

Linda **has painted** a picture. You **have** it.

PRACTICE

(Written) Write the complete verbs. Circle the helping verbs.

Example: We have worked hard.
(have) worked

1. May has cut two circles.
2. They are making pinwheels.
3. He has lost the yo-yo!
4. They will park the car.
5. My cup is falling.

WORD BANK	
is	are
has	have
was	were
am	had
will	would

APPLY

Write three sentences with helping verbs.

Irregular Verbs:
Think, Eat, Sit

> ***Think, eat,*** and ***sit*** are ***irregular verbs.*** You do not add ***-ed*** to form the past tense.
>
> think→thought   eat→ate   sit→sat

Verbs can show time. A verb that tells about the past is in the *past tense.* To form the past tense of most verbs, add *-ed.*

You do not add *-ed* to form the past tense of *irregular verbs.* You must change the whole verb. How does the verb *sit* change in these examples?

I **sit** in the red chair.
I **sat** there in the morning, too.
I **have sat** there all week.

See how each verb changes.

Irregular Verbs

Present	Past	Past with Helping Verb
think	thought	have thought, has thought
eat	ate	have eaten, has eaten
sit	sat	have sat, has sat

PRACTICE

A. (Oral) Tell the correct verb for each sentence. Use the chart if you need help.

> **Example:** Yesterday I (<u>sit/sat</u>) in that chair.
> **sat**

1. Today Sandy (<u>thinks/thought</u>) it will rain.
2. If you whistle now, the dog (<u>sits/sat</u>).
3. Now I make sure I (<u>ate/eat</u>) a good lunch.
4. Last night we (<u>think/thought</u>) of a good idea.
5. Yesterday Sara (<u>ate/eats</u>) corn on the cob.
6. All last summer it (<u>sit/sat</u>) in that boat.

B. (Written) Write the correct verb for each sentence.

1. We (<u>has thought/have thought</u>) of everything!
2. That silly cat (<u>sat/sit</u>) on the step all day yesterday.
3. Yesterday Yen Yen (<u>thought/think</u>) she was sick.
4. I (<u>has eaten/have eaten</u>) many good meals at Nick's house.
5. Grandma (<u>has sat/sits</u>) next to me now.
6. The whole team (<u>ate/eat</u>) the same lunch yesterday.

APPLY

Suppose you had to plan breakfast for ten people. Write three sentences about it. Use forms of the verbs *eat* and *think*.

Review the Basics I

A. Matching Subjects and Verbs
Write the correct verb for each sentence. *(pages 228–229)*

1. Cathy (is/am) the youngest in her family.
2. Still, everyone (depend/depends) on her.
3. Her family (take/takes) trips together.
4. On every trip, Cathy (carry/carries) the camera.
5. The camera (are/is) only a small one.
6. Even so, the pictures (are/is) in color.
7. After the trip, her sisters (pick/picks) the best ones.
8. Sometimes the pictures (are/is) funny.
9. The girls (like/likes) them.

B. Matching Pronouns and Verbs
Write the correct verb for each sentence. *(pages 230–231)*

1. This afternoon we (bake/bakes) the bread.
2. You (measure/measures) everything.
3. Here, it (hold/holds) one cup.
4. He (say/says) we need two and a half cups.
5. Now they (fill/fills) the cup twice.
6. Each time, we (dump/dumps) the flour in the bowl.
7. After that, she (fill/fills) it half full.
8. I (add/adds) that to the two cups in the bowl.
9. I (love/loves) fresh bread.

C. Using *Has* and *Have*

Write *has* or *have* for each sentence. *(page 232)*

1. Yes, I (has/have) keys of all kinds.
2. They (has/have) such different shapes.
3. Look, this one (has/have) a crack in it.
4. My dad (has/have) a key chain for me.
5. We (has/have) time to shine them now.

D. Helping Verbs

Write the complete verbs. Circle the helping verbs. *(page 233)*

1. You have made a wonderful model.
2. This year I have tried to make some, too.
3. Carlos has built some from kits.
4. Gary is putting those two together.
5. I am making one from toothpicks.

E. Irregular Verbs

Write the correct verb for each sentence. *(pages 234–235)*

1. All last week we (sit/sat) on boxes.
2. I (eat/ate) the tomato soup now.
3. Last night Sven (thinks/thought) he had lost his puppy.
4. Right now Alice (sits/sat) in front of me.
5. Randy (thinks/thought) we can jump now.
6. Did you see what I (eat/ate) for lunch yesterday?

Verbs in a Paragraph

You have learned many things about verbs. You know that verbs must match their subjects. You also know that verbs can show time. For most verbs, you add *-ed* to show past tense. Irregular verbs, such as *sit* and *think,* change in the past tense *(sat, thought).* Remember that some verbs are main verbs and some are helping verbs.

Look at these sentences.

Lisa **has** a friend.
Lisa **has found** a new friend.

In the first sentence, *has* is a main verb. What kind of verb is *has* in the second sentence?

Read the Reminders.

REMINDERS

1. Use the *s*-form with subjects that mean *he, she,* or *it.*

2. For most verbs, add *-ed* to form the past tense. Irregular verbs may change completely in the past tense.

3. Helping verbs must match their subjects. Use *has* with subjects that mean *he, she,* or *it.* Use *have* with *I* and subjects that mean *we, you,* or *they.*

You use many kinds of verbs in a paragraph. Look at the verbs in this paragraph.

In the past, many people have lived on farms. Pigs ate most of the garbage. Farmers buried the rest. Today, though, garbage is a problem. More people are living in America. Each person throws away more than a pound of garbage every day.

Which two verbs in the paragraph match singular subjects? Find the helping verbs. How many are there? Do you see irregular verbs?

PRACTICE/APPLY

A. **(Written)** Write the verb or verbs in each sentence. Draw a line under the helping verbs.

Example: 2. have burned

(1) Wastepaper is a problem. (2) People have burned it. (3) People have buried it. (4) Now they are thinking. (5) They reuse it. (6) They have made wastepaper useful!

B. **(Written)** Write the following paragraph. Use the correct verb forms.

I (has/have) wondered about other planets. In the past, I (think/thought) they were far away. Now our country (has/have) sent spaceships to Mars. We (sat/sit) and watched the pictures.

Punctuating Conversations

When people talk to each other, they have a conversation. You read conversations in stories. You can write conversations, too.

Every written conversation has two parts. One part is what the person says. That part is the *quotation*. What the person says always has *quotation marks* around it. The first word in the quotation begins with a capital letter.

A conversation has another part, too. That part is called the *speaker tag*. The speaker tag tells who is talking. Put a punctuation mark between the quotation and the speaker tag. Use a comma if the speaker tag comes before the words of the speaker.

Look at the punctuation marks in this talk.

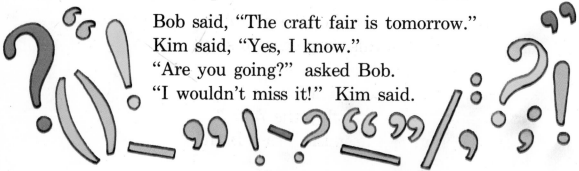

Bob said, "The craft fair is tomorrow."
Kim said, "Yes, I know."
"Are you going?" asked Bob.
"I wouldn't miss it!" Kim said.

What did Bob say in the first sentence? How can you tell? Where is the speaker tag in each sentence? What punctuation follows it?

Who asked the question? How do you know? Name the speakers in the above conversation.

PRACTICE

A. (Oral) Tell the words that are the speaker tags.

> **Example:** Kim said, "Is Pete here?"
> **Kim said,**

1. "Here I am," Pete said.
2. Kim said, "Did you bring your coins?"
3. Pete answered, "Yes, I did."
4. Amy said, "They are pretty!"
5. "Thank you," said Pete.
6. Amy said, "Those coins are square!"
7. "They are from India," explained Pete.
8. Kim said, "I like the coins with holes."

B. (Written) Each sentence has one mistake. Write each sentence correctly.

> **Example:** Beth asked, "do I hear music?"
> **Beth asked, "Do I hear music"**

1. Jeff said "I love to play the piano!"
2. Tom asked, "Is this song easy to sing?
3. Katy replied, I think it is."
4. "Look at me! shouted Michelle.
5. Wing said, "she can play the flute."
6. "let's march to the music," said Beth.

APPLY

Write a short conversation between a cartoon character and yourself. Put the speaker tag first in each sentence.

Reasons

People have different feelings. They may feel happy one day. They may feel sad the next day. These are not the only feelings they can have.

Look at this list of words.

happy	pleased	thrilled	worried
sad	brave	upset	surprised

Each word describes a feeling. There are many other words that describe feelings, too.

Often you can find the reason a person feels a certain way.

Look at these paragraphs.

It was summer. No rain had fallen for weeks. Mr. Owens looked at his crops. They were too dry. The corn would die if rain did not fall soon. The farmer smiled up at the rain clouds.

Tina Owens whistled. Today was the big picnic. It was the last time this summer she would see her friends. Tina frowned when she saw the rain clouds.

How did Mr. Owens feel when he saw the rain clouds? Give the reason he might have felt that way. How did Tina feel? Why did she feel that way?

PRACTICE

A. (Oral) Tell how each person might feel.

> **Example:** Chris was once scratched by a cat. Now a strange cat jumps in her lap.
> **afraid, scared**

1. Manny is trying to catch the school bus. His brother is packing their lunches very slowly.
2. Ellen loves dogs. She gets a puppy for her birthday.
3. Harry likes to sing. He is picked to sing a solo.
4. It is Jill's first day at the new school. She is looking for her classroom, but the doors all look the same.
5. Amalia is lost. She sees her aunt across the street.

B. (Written) Write these three headings.

Person   Feeling   Reason

Look at the picture. On your paper, write how each person feels. Give a reason for the feeling.

APPLY

You have won three games in a row. Write a sentence. Tell how you feel. Give reasons.

Causes

Sometimes something happens because something else happened first. The first action *caused* the second one. When you know the cause, you know why something happened.

Look at these sentences.

> Carmen **dropped** the camera.
> The camera **broke.**

The first sentence tells why the camera broke. It broke because Carmen dropped it. Dropping it caused it to break.

One action does not always cause another action. Two actions may just happen at the same time.

Look at these sentences.

> The woman at the store fixed the camera.
> She sells good cameras.

When you see the word *because,* you know one action is a cause.

Look at these sentences.

> I got wet **because** it was raining.
> The team got better **because** it worked hard.

What is the action in each? What is the cause?

PRACTICE

A. (Oral) Read the sentence pairs. Tell if the action in the second sentence in each pair was caused by the first. In some sentences there may be no cause for the action.

> **Example:** He dropped his glasses. The glasses broke.
> **action was caused**

1. The glue spilled. The table got sticky.
2. The glue was lost. We painted the sky blue.
3. Alan followed directions. He built a good model.
4. Pam bought paint. She saw a bus.
5. The model plane ran out of fuel. It stopped flying.
6. Yesterday it rained. We did not play outside.

B. (Written) Write an action that might happen because of each sentence.

> **Example:** I let go of the kite string.
> **The kite flew away.**

1. The alarm clock rang.
2. Luis carried three eggs in one hand.
3. I rode my bike over a nail.
4. Robin forgot her spelling book.
5. The pen ran out of ink.
6. John's father hugged him.

APPLY

Suppose you could fly. Write three sentences. Tell what might happen.

Irregular Verbs:
Take, See, Come

> ***Take, see,*** and ***come*** are ***irregular verbs.*** **You do not add *-ed* to show past tense.**
>
> I <u>see</u> it. I <u>saw</u> it yesterday. I <u>have seen</u> it many times.

You know that verbs can show time. A verb that shows past time is in the past tense.

Look at these two sets of sentences.

> She **took** two pieces before.
> She **has taken** enough.

> Yesterday she **mixed** red and yellow.
> All the pupils **have mixed** paints.

Name the irregular verb. Name the helping verbs.

See how each verb changes.

Irregular Verbs

Present	Past	Past with Helping Verb
take	took	has taken, have taken
see	saw	has seen, have seen
come	came	has come, have come

PRACTICE

A. (Oral) Tell the correct verb for each sentence. Use the chart if you need help.

> **Example:** Last month Marco (sees/saw) a deer.
> **saw**

1. Now Don (took/takes) his clothes upstairs!
2. Now Lai Ling (sees/saw) the rain.
3. Last week, Rita (came/comes) to my house.
4. Yesterday you (took/takes) that bag home.
5. I (see/saw) what you mean now.
6. Now Omar (came/comes) on my bus.
7. Yesterday Tony (took/takes) his radio with him.
8. Joan (came/comes) to visit last week.

B. (Written) Write the correct verb for each sentence.

1. Our sister (has seen/have seen) many movies.
2. Yesterday Hector (comes/came) home.
3. I (took/has taken) the spelling test last week.
4. Paul and Mark (has come/have come) to school.
5. Marion (saw/sees) this fish now.
6. Yesterday we (saw/see) gulls at the beach.
7. The dog (has taken/have taken) my sandwich!

APPLY

Imagine you were offered a crayon or a yo-yo. Write two sentences telling which you took. Use the past tense of *take, see,* or *come.*

The Verb *Do*

> **The verb *do* is an irregular verb.**
> do   did   have done

In the present tense, the verb *do* is like many verbs.

Look at these examples.

> **I|do** my best work in the morning.
> **Tom|does** his best work in the morning, too.
> Sometimes **we|do** our work together.

Why is the *s*-form used in the second sentence?

Do is an irregular verb. It changes in the past tense.

Look at these sentences.

> Last week **I did** a good job. **Gail did,** too.
> **We did** something silly also. **I have done**
>   something silly often.

What form of *do* is used with a helping verb?

Forms of Verb *Do*

Subjects	Present	Past	Past with Helping Verb
I, you, we, they she, he, it	do does	did did	have done has done

PRACTICE

A. (Oral) Tell the correct verb for each sentence. Use the chart if you need help.

> **Example:** Last summer, Maria (does/did) me a favor.
> **did**

1. At parties we (do/does) magic tricks.
2. You (do/does) the best magic trick.
3. Eliot (have done/has done) only simple tricks.
4. The workers (do/did) the job last week.
5. Ralph (has done/have done) an odd picture.
6. Ellen (do/does) the job well!
7. Police officers really (do/does) hard work.

B. (Written) Decide which form of *do* completes each sentence. Write the verbs.

> **Example:** My pen _____ work now.
> **does**

1. Yesterday, the puppy _____ something new.
2. You have _____ a good job.
3. Now the clown _____ another act.
4. Last week we _____ the dishes.
5. Now I _____ all the cooking.
6. The ranger has _____ a great job.

APPLY

Write three sentences about a magic show. What does everyone do? Use a form of the verb *do* in each sentence.

Contractions with *Not*

> A *contraction* is a short way of writing two words. An *apostrophe* (') is always used in a contraction.
>
> did + not = didn't   was + not = wasn't

A contraction is made from two words. The words are joined and letters are dropped. An apostrophe (') shows where letters were dropped.

Look at these contractions.

> are not = aren't   have not = haven't
> is not = isn't   was not = wasn't

What letter was dropped from each?

Sometimes more than one letter is dropped. Sometimes the word changes completely.

Look at these examples.

> cannot = can't   will not = won't

Which word changes when it is used in a contraction? How many letters were dropped from the other contraction?

What words are joined in each contraction?

> isn't   hasn't   don't   doesn't   wasn't
> aren't   haven't didn't can't   won't

PRACTICE

A. (Oral) Say the contraction in each sentence.

> **Example:** We didn't find them.
> **didn't**

1. Please don't forget to save bottle caps.
2. Tim doesn't have a blue one yet.
3. Of course, he hasn't been saving long.
4. Pretty caps aren't easy to find.
5. Saving common ones isn't much fun.
6. A collection won't look good that way.
7. It isn't hard to save them.

B. (Written) Write contractions for the underlined words.

> **Example:** I do not have the film.
> **don't**

1. My friends cannot wait to see these pictures!
2. Tony and Phil will not move.
3. They do not know where you are.
4. Wait, the light is not bright enough.
5. Good, the camera has not moved.
6. You have not taken my picture.
7. My friends will not see me.

APPLY

Write three sentences about a broken bike. Use a contraction in each one.

Avoiding Double Negatives

> **A word that means "no" or "not" is called a *negative word*. Do not use two negative words in the same sentence.**
> Incorrect: There are not no pears left.
> Correct: There are not any pears left.
> Or: There are no pears left.

Negative words mean "no" or "not."

Look at the negative words in the Word Bank.

Contractions can be negative, too. If one of the words is *not,* the contraction is negative.

Here are some negative contractions.

isn't   can't   doesn't   aren't

Two negative words should not be used in one sentence. Use either one negative word or one negative contraction.

Look at these examples.

Daryl **has no** pets.
Daryl **hasn't any** pets.
I **can never** remember names.
I **can't ever** remember names.

What are the negative words or contractions?

WORD BANK

Negative Words

no
nobody
none
never
no one
nothing
nowhere
not

PRACTICE

A. (Oral) Tell the correct word to complete each sentence.

Example: Pablo didn't bring (<u>any</u>/no) lunch.
any

1. A few birds don't (<u>never/ever</u>) fly.
2. Maureen has not bought (<u>no/any</u>) presents yet.
3. Now Alicia hasn't (<u>no/any</u>) money left.
4. Did you know there (<u>is/isn't</u>) no ham in hamburger?
5. I didn't call (<u>anybody/nobody</u>) yesterday.
6. Tanya and I aren't going (<u>anywhere/nowhere</u>).
7. On Saturday no one (<u>can/can't</u>) come.

B. (Written) Write the negative word in each sentence.

Example: Donna doesn't watch TV.
doesn't

1. Donna's parents don't own a TV.
2. They have none at all.
3. They have never owned one.
4. Donna said no one even misses it.
5. Few homes in this country have no TV.
6. We don't need a TV set.

APPLY

Write three sentences about a make-believe person named Ed. Ed has none of the things you have. Use a negative word in each sentence.

Review the Basics II

A. Irregular Verbs: *Take, See, Come*
Write the correct verb for each sentence. *(pages 246–247)*

1. Yesterday Bruce (takes/took) his bag.
2. Don (have come/has come) to visit us.
3. You can now (see/saw) the island clearly.
4. Both children (has taken/have taken) their gloves.
5. Last week I (saw/see) kittens in that store.
6. Now Dave (takes/took) another card.
7. Last summer we (came/come) by boat.
8. That raccoon (comes/came) every evening now.
9. We (has seen/have seen) the whale!
10. Last fall I (took/take) art classes.

B. The Verb *Do*
Write the correct verb for each sentence. *(pages 248–249)*

1. My dog (did/does) that trick yesterday.
2. You (does/do) it alone now.
3. Now my sister (does/do) her work.
4. My cousin (do/does) the yard.
5. Yesterday they really (did/do) a good job.
6. The group has (done/did) four songs together.
7. Now I can (do/does) it perfectly.
8. We have (did/done) everything wrong!

C. Contractions with *Not*
Write contractions for the underlined words.
(pages 250–251)

1. A dollar bill <u>does not</u> last long.
2. It <u>is not</u> very strong.
3. Old money <u>cannot</u> be thrown out.
4. The government <u>will not</u> do that.
5. The bills <u>are not</u> hidden either.
6. They are burned so people <u>cannot</u> use them.
7. Big bills <u>are not</u> made often.
8. After all, they <u>do not</u> get much use.
9. Our money <u>does not</u> wear out.
10. It <u>will not</u> stay with us long enough!

D. Avoiding Double Negatives
Choose the correct word to complete each sentence. *(pages 252–253)*

1. Many people haven't (<u>never/ever</u>) been to another planet.
2. Long ago spaceships didn't carry (<u>anybody/nobody</u>).
3. No one has (<u>ever/never</u>) flown to the sun.
4. The space shuttle didn't go (<u>nowhere/anywhere</u>) new.
5. Still, it returned with (<u>no/any</u>) cracks or breaks.
6. There was (<u>nothing/anything</u>) important broken.
7. We won't need (<u>no/any</u>) new rocket for another trip.
8. The country has (<u>no/any</u>) need for one.

Story Parts

All good stories are alike in four ways. They have *characters* and a *setting*. They have a *problem* and a *solution* to the problem. These are called story parts.

The *characters* are the people or animals in the story. One story might be about a boy named Joe.

The *setting* is the place where the story takes place. It is also the time when the story takes place. Joe lives on a farm in Ohio. The time is July of this year.

A Birthday Present

Joe has a problem. Tomorrow is his father's birthday. Joe does not have a present for him. Then Joe hears Dad talk about the goats' dirty pen. Dad says he wishes he had more time. He wants to clean the pen.

Joe thinks how to solve his *problem*. He thinks of a *solution*. Joe writes Dad a note. The note promises Dad a clean goats' pen that day.

GUIDELINES

1. Each story should have four parts.
2. The story parts are characters, setting, problem, and solution.

PRACTICE

A. (Written) Write the names of the four story parts. Write *Characters, Setting, Problem,* and *Solution.* One part is missing from this story. Circle the name of the missing part.

Myra's Cape

Myra lived long ago. She lived in a small town. Her school was a long walk from home. Myra was very worried on the way to school. It was snowy and cold. There was the schoolhouse! She ran inside. She was happy to see her cape. It was hanging on a hook.

B. (Written) Write the names of the story parts. A part is missing here. Circle it.

A Helpful Neighbor

Teresa walks to the next block to wait for the school bus. Suddenly, she hears a loud meow! Her new kitten has followed her to the bus stop. The school bus is coming soon. Then Teresa sees her neighbor, Mr. Wheeler. He just bought a newspaper at the corner store. He is walking back to his house.

APPLY

Think of a story you like. Write three sentences about the setting.

Story Beginnings and Endings

A story has characters and a setting. It has a problem and a solution.

Read the story.

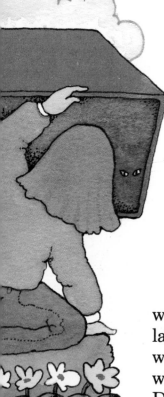

The Tale of the Missing Cat

Jan lives in a small house on a busy street. She has a small cat named Aggy. Aggy has a very long bushy tail.

Last Tuesday, Jan couldn't find Aggy. She looked in Aggy's hiding places. Aggy wasn't under a bed. She wasn't on the shelf in the hall. Jan went out on the porch. She looked into the backyard. She saw a large box that had fallen over. The box began to move. Something was inside the box. Jan looked. She had found Aggy at last.

Look back at the title. It is written in a special way. Often a title is not a sentence. The first and last words start with capital letters. All important words in titles start with capital letters, too. See which words of the title begin with a capital letter. Does it give you a clue to what the story is about? How does the story end? What problem is solved?

PRACTICE

A. (Oral) Read the sentences. Tell the ones that
might be story beginnings. Tell the sentences
that might be story endings.

1. Kevin walked up to his house. The police officer had
been a big help.

   Kevin had just moved to Dixon Street. He wanted to
take a walk. He hoped he wouldn't get lost.

2. It was pouring rain. Gladys was afraid the party would
be spoiled.

   The party was lots of fun. Grandfather had saved the
day by making a tent.

B. (Written) Study the picture. Imagine a story
about it. Write a title. Remember to use
capital letters.

Example: An Unusual Picnic

APPLY

Write two sentences that could begin a story.

A Story: Plan, Write, Edit

Do you remember the four parts of a story? You often meet the characters early in the story. The author tells the setting at the start, too. Near the start, you learn the problem. The ending tells how the problem was solved. The solution always comes at the end.

PLAN

Plan your story first. Use the picture of the beach. Choose something in the picture to write about.

Think about the four story parts. Make a list of notes for them. A list will help you write your story.

> **Characters:** Who are the people?
> **Setting:** What kind of day is it? Where is the place? What is it like?
> **Problem:** What is the problem going to be? Make it a good one.
> **Solution:** How is it solved?

Think of a good title for your story. Does it give a clue about the story?

You now have a list of the important parts of the story. Your list will help you write your story. Use your notes.

WRITE

Now write your story. Begin by introducing the characters. Describe the setting. Then tell what the problem is. How do the characters solve the problem?

Remember these Guidelines.

GUIDELINES

1. Write the story title correctly. Use capital letters where needed.
2. Introduce the characters.
3. Describe when and where the story takes place. This is the setting.
4. Describe the problem.
5. Tell how the characters solve the problem.

EDIT

Now you have finished the story. You are ready to edit it. First practice editing on this story. Rewrite it with the three mistakes fixed. One sentence has too many negative words. A contraction needs to be fixed. There is a story part missing. Add it.

What about Tiger?

Jane and Dan drove to the beach with their parents. When they got to the beach, they couldn't find no leash for their dog, Tiger.

Everyone was upset. They wanted to spend the day. They couldnt leave Tiger in the car. Dogs shouldn't run loose on the beach.

Jane and Dan talked all the way home. It had been a wonderful day on the beach. Tiger joined their talk. He barked once. He had had a good day on the beach, too.

Edit your story. Use these Guidelines.

GUIDELINES

1. Write an interesting title.
2. Make sure you have a setting and characters.
3. Include a problem. Give the solution.
4. Use apostrophes in contractions correctly.
5. Fix any double negatives.

After you edit your story, copy it in your best handwriting.

17 COMMUNICATING

Telling a Story

Telling a story is like giving a talk. It is easy to tell a story aloud. But you must be prepared. Write notes to help you remember your story.

Write short notes about each story part. Tell about the characters and the setting. Decide on a problem. Note how the characters solve it.

Use the Guidelines.

GUIDELINES

1. Make notes about your story. Write short notes for each story part.
2. Use your story notes. Tell your story in order.
3. Speak loudly and clearly but not too fast. Look at your listeners while you speak.

PRACTICE/APPLY

(Oral) Tell a story to the class. Tell the story you wrote for Lesson 16. If you want, make up a new story to tell.

Unit 6 Test

A. Matching Subjects and Verbs
Write the correct verb for each sentence. *(pages 228–231)*

1. Tomato farming (is/are) a big business.
2. Machines (do/does) much of the work.
3. A plow (break/breaks) the ground before planting.
4. Planters (drop/drops) seed and plant food in even rows.
5. Large sprinklers (water/waters) the little plants.
6. Each plant (grow/grows) fast.

B. Using *Has* and *Have*
Write *has* or *have* for each sentence. *(page 232)*

1. We (has/have) a new project.
2. The teacher (has/have) food charts on the board.
3. We (have/has) pictures of food groups.
4. Jack (have/has) the pictures of fruits.
5. Ana (has/have) the pictures of meats.
6. One picture (has/have) a torn corner!

C. Helping Verbs
Write the complete verbs. Circle the helping verbs. *(page 233)*

1. Dr. Tripp is talking to our class.
2. The doctor has spoken here before.
3. In other years I have listened to him.
4. Today Dr. Tripp is talking about eye patches.

5. Eye patches are helping many people.

6. Doctors have tested our eyes.

D. Irregular Verbs
Write the correct verb. *(pages 234–235, 246–249)*

1. Last week Leslie (sit/sat) in front of me.

2. Now the bird (took/takes) a sunflower seed.

3. We have (did/done) our best.

4. Yesterday at the pond, we (see/saw) fish.

5. We (eat/ate) cheese for lunch yesterday.

6. Now you (think/thought) of a joke to tell me.

E. Contractions with *Not*
Write contractions for the underlined words.
(pages 250–251)

1. I have not seen a real comet.

2. Bright ones do not appear often.

3. People will not see every comet.

4. Many are not very bright.

5. You cannot see some with just your eyes.

6. One comet is not expected for 500 years.

F. Writing
Write a short story. Make sure your story beginning has a setting. Describe a problem the characters have. Tell how the problem is solved. Give your story a title. *(pages 260–262)*

Keep Practicing

A. Pronouns

Find the subject of each sentence. Decide which pronoun should stand for it. Write the pronoun.
(Unit 5, Lesson 1)

1. José, Mom, and I made popcorn.
2. Popcorn is a good snack.
3. José poured the popcorn into a big bowl.
4. Mom explained the popping.
5. The pieces of corn have water inside.
6. At first the water is cold.
7. Then people heat the corn.
8. The water turns to steam.
9. The popcorn is blown up by steam.

B. More Pronouns

Read each sentence and decide which pronoun is correct. Write the pronoun. *(Unit 5, Lesson 2)*

1. Ida gave (he/him) two apples.
2. Ted ate (they/them).
3. The apples tasted good to (us/we).
4. Later the dentist talked to (we/us).
5. Dr. Smith told (I/me) about apples.
6. "Apples are good for (she/her)," said Dr. Smith.
7. We will bring some with (us/we).
8. I will give one to (she/her).
9. The other one is for (he/him).

C. Using *I* or *Me*
Decide which pronoun should complete each sentence. Write the pronoun. *(Unit 5, Lesson 3)*

1. My sister and (I/me) finally did it!
2. Katy and (I/me) taught Sparky a word.
3. My folks gave Sparky to (I/me).
4. (I/Me) have always wanted a parrot.
5. For months (I/me) talked to Sparky.
6. Now Sparky talks to Katy and (I/me).
7. At first Sparky just looked at (I/me).
8. For weeks (I/me) said, "Pretty bird."
9. Then Sparky said it back to (I/me).

D. Contractions with Pronouns
Decide how to change each pronoun and verb to a contraction. Write sentences using the contraction. *(Unit 5, Lesson 9)*

1. Finally you are ready.
2. She will carry the net.
3. Dina says it is slippery.
4. He has brought the buttons.
5. They had checked the tickets!
6. Thursday I am arriving late.
7. We have made the salad.
8. Alex said he would fix it.
9. Yes, it will wait.

E. Too Many Nouns

Read each pair of sentences. Rewrite the second sentence. Use a pronoun in place of the repeated word or words. *(Unit 5, Lesson 10)*

1. A robin is a nice bird. <u>A robin</u> is brown and orange.
2. This bird has a pretty song. <u>This bird</u> sings a lot.
3. Robins build big, strong nests. <u>Robins</u> work hard at it.
4. A nest is made of twigs, grass, and mud. <u>A nest</u> can have other things in it, too.
5. The mother robin lays three to five eggs. <u>The mother robin</u> sits on them.
6. The eggs hatch. <u>The eggs</u> held baby robins.
7. The father robin guards the nest. <u>The father robin</u> brings food, too.
8. The babies try to fly. At last <u>the babies</u> do it.
9. My friend and I watched them. <u>My friend and I</u> like robins.

F. Too Many Pronouns

Read the sentences. In four sentences, pronouns should be dropped. Fix those sentences. *(Unit 5, Lesson 11)*

1. A quarter it is called "two bits."
2. People they used that name for years.
3. A man he might have one coin.
4. That person probably cut it into pieces.
5. You and I we use small coins.

G. Facts
Write the facts. *(Unit 5, Lesson 6)*

1. Yarn can be made into cloth.
2. Peanuts are delicious.
3. Everyone loves peanut butter.
4. Tuesday is the day after Monday.
5. Ten cents is more than five cents.

H. Opinions
There are three opinions listed below. Write the sentences that are opinions. *(Unit 5, Lesson 7)*

1. Airplanes are faster than cars.
2. Red is the best color.
3. Photographs are better than drawings.
4. Apples grow on trees.
5. Apples are better than oranges.

I. Words That Persuade
Write each word. Then circle the words that would persuade you to like something. *(Unit 5, Lesson 8)*

1. cheerful
2. broken
3. happy
4. sweet
5. bad
6. friendly
7. ugly
8. beautiful
9. good
10. messy
11. nice
12. lumpy
13. brave
14. cozy
15. awful

Something Extra

You Don't Say!

A circus is in town! The children in the picture are at the circus. They are watching an act in the center ring. The people in the act are high above the ground. Do the children have the same feelings and thoughts? Do they all like the act?

Read the sentences in the picture. They will tell you what three of the children are thinking.

Oh no! I'm afraid something terrible will happen. It is scary how swiftly they swing. Watch out!

I want some popcorn. It smells delicious. Do I have enough money? I'll count it.

I wonder if there will be more trained animal acts. I liked the dancing bears. I think I see the seals coming in down there.

Who is thinking each group of thoughts? How do you know? Both the words and the picture help you to decide. Match three of the children with their thoughts.

Write Away!

There is a fourth child in the picture. Look at her face. Look at how she is sitting. Write what she may be thinking. Give your readers a clear word picture! Here are some ideas to help you start.

exciting show   bright, fancy costumes

brave flyers   scary leaps and twirls

Dictionary

A dictionary's where you can look things up
    To see if they're really there:
        To see if what you breathe is AIR,
        If what you sit on is a CHAIR,
        If what you comb is curly HAIR,
        If what you drink from is a CUP.
A dictionary's where you can look things up
    To see if they're really there.

—*William Jay Smith*

7

Making
Reports

Review: Sentences

> **The first word in a *sentence* begins with a capital letter. It ends with a punctuation mark.**

Remember that a sentence that tells something is a *statement*. A sentence that asks something is a *question*. A sentence that shows strong feeling is an *exclamation*.

Look at these sentences.

> Deaf people can use the phone.
> How do they know when someone is calling?
> They use a special machine!

Which sentence is a statement? Which is a question? Which is an exclamation?

Remember that the subject tells whom or what.

Find the subjects in these sentences.

> Maria's phone has a light.
> The light flashes.
> Maria picks up the phone.

The predicate tells more about the subject. It may tell about an action. It may tell what the subject is, does, or has. Look at the examples above again. Find the predicate in each.

If you need more help with the Practice, look back at pages 12–15 and 28–31.

PRACTICE

A. (Written) Copy the sentences. Draw a line between the subject and the predicate.

> **Example:** Inez turned on the heater.
> **Inez|turned on the heater.**

1. Augusta Rogers lived in Brooklyn.
2. She was an inventor.
3. This woman invented a heater.
4. The heater warmed cars.
5. Cars have heaters now.
6. People can ride in warm cars.

B. (Written) Each sentence has a mistake. Fix each one. Write the sentences.

> **Example:** there are many kinds of machines.
> **There are many kinds of machines.**

7. maria has a machine.
8. it attaches to the phone.
9. What does the machine do
10. Maria cannot hear voices
11. this machine types people's words.

APPLY

What tool do you use? Write a statement about it. Then write a question and an exclamation.

Review: Nouns

> A *noun* is a word that names a person, place, or thing. A *singular noun* names one thing. A *plural noun* names more than one.

Look at the chart for examples.

Singular and Plural Nouns

Singular	cat	glass	dish	family	child
Plural	cats	glasses	dishes	families	children

To make most plural nouns, you can just add *-s* or *-es.* For others, you need to use special rules. What is the plural of *puppy* or *mouse?*

You know that there are *common nouns* and *proper nouns.* Proper nouns name special people, places, or things. They begin with capital letters.

Look at this chart for examples.

Common and Proper Nouns

Common	dog	day	city	street	month
Proper	Rover	Monday	Denver	Main Street	July

If you need more help with the Practice, look back at pages 54–61.

PRACTICE

A. (Written) Write the plural form of each noun.

Example: box
boxes

1. party	7. beach	13. tooth
2. bush	8. country	14. parade
3. six	9. dress	15. hat
4. candle	10. gift	16. cake
5. city	11. kite	17. puppy
6. goose	12. week	18. mouse

B. (Written) Write each sentence correctly.

Example: My birthday is in june.
My birthday is in June.

19. My best friend is named ben.
20. We both go to jefferson school.
21. It is on oak street.
22. On tuesday we studied holidays.
23. One was new year's day.
24. In one country, it comes in april.

APPLY

Make up a funny animal. Write three sentences about it. Tell its name, where it lives, and what it does. Draw a line under each noun.

Review: Verbs

> **A verb form can show *present, past,* or *future tense.* The verb form must match its subject.**

Verbs in the *present tense* tell what is happening now. Remember to use the *s*-form only if the subject means *she, he,* or *it.*

Look at this example.

The teacher **tells** about a party.

Verbs in the *past tense* tell what happened. Verbs in the *future tense* tell what will happen.

Look at these examples.

The class **cooked.** We **will have** a party.

You know that a verb must match its subject. Do not use the *s*-form of the verb with *I.*

Look at these sentences.

I **am** making a piñata. **I like** piñatas.

Do not use the *s*-form of the verb with plural subjects. These mean *we, you,* or *they.*

Here are two examples.

We **make** a clown. Ed and Sherry **fill** it.

If you need more help with the Practice, look back at pages 100–105 and 114–117.

PRACTICE

A. (Written) Use the tense at the end of each sentence. Write the correct form of each verb.

> **Example:** We (fill) the piñata with peanuts. (past)
> **filled**

1. Estella (put) on the blindfold first. (future)
2. You (turn) her around and around. (present)
3. Now Estella (swing) the stick. (future)
4. Earlier I (try) to break the piñata. (past)
5. Finally the stick (hit) it! (present)
6. The peanuts (tumble) everywhere. (past)

B. (Written) Write the correct verb form.

> **Example:** People in this country (like/likes) holidays.
> **like**

7. One favorite holiday (come/comes) in February.
8. On February we (wait/waits) for a groundhog.
9. The shadow of the animal (is/are) important.
10. I (is/am) not sure the animal is always right.
11. Sandy (believe/believes) it.

APPLY

Write three sentences telling what you enjoy doing on a holiday. Draw a line under each verb.

Review: Adjectives

An *adjective* adds details. Adjectives can be used to compare things, too.

An adjective tells about a noun.

Look at the adjectives in these sentences.

Fred looks into the **big, white** pot.
The **hot** cider has a **spicy** smell.

Which adjectives tell about size? Color? Which adjectives add details about what you feel or smell?

Adjectives can help you compare things, too. Add -*er* to some adjectives to compare two things. For other adjectives, the word *more* is used.

Look at these examples.

Crane Farm cider is **sweeter** than ours.
This is **more delicious** than cold cider.

Compare three or more things by using the ending -*est*. For some adjectives, use the word *most*.

Look at the adjectives in these sentences.

That is the **tastiest** drink of all!
This room is the **most comfortable** in the inn.

When is the ending -*est* used? When is *most* used?

If you need more help with the Practice, look back at pages 140–147.

PRACTICE

A. (Written) Find the adjective and its noun in each sentence. Write them.

> **Example:** We like to drink fresh cider.
> **fresh cider**

1. We grow good apples on our farm.
2. Do you see the little trees on the hill?
3. Juicy apples grow on them.
4. We put the ripe fruit in baskets.
5. Perfect apples are saved.
6. Bruised fruit is crushed.
7. It becomes sweet cider.

B. (Written) Write each adjective. Write the forms used to compare two things and three or more things.

> **Examples: large   larger   largest**
> **wonderful   more wonderful   most wonderful**

8. tiny	**12.** hot	**16.** wet
9. beautiful	**13.** mysterious	**17.** cold
10. old	**14.** silly	**18.** important
11. soft	**15.** pretty	**19.** happy

APPLY

What is very sticky or very soft? Write three sentences describing it. Use an adjective in each.

Review: Adverbs

> An *adverb* tells where, when, or how. It may tell more about a verb.

An adverb may tell about a verb. It may tell where something is done. It may tell when or how it happened.

Which words do these adverbs tell about?

Trucks go **everywhere.** (Where?)
They carry heavy loads **easily.** (How?)
Animals **often** carry big loads. (When?)

To find adverbs, you know to ask yourself three questions. Where? When? How? You also know one more clue. Adverbs often end in *-ly*.

Look at the chart for some examples.

Adverbs

Where		When		How
there	here	soon	later	carefully
far	near	then	now	silently
above	below	first	next	happily
outside	inside	early	lately	gladly
nowhere	everywhere	sometime		softly

If you need more help with the Practice, look back at pages 158–165.

PRACTICE

A. (Written) Find the adverb and its verb in each sentence. Write them.

> **Example:** The bus stops slowly.
> **stops slowly**

1. Cars move smoothly.
2. Some people rarely use roads.
3. Boats travel easily.
4. Water taxis move quickly.
5. Water is everywhere.

B. (Written) Add adverbs that answer the questions.

> **Example:** We cheered _____ . (How?)
> **We cheered loudly.**

  6. He dances _____ . (How?)
  7. I looked _____ for my hat. (Where?)
  8. The baby went to sleep _____ . (When?)
  9. We sang _____ . (How?)
10. We are going to the store _____ . (When?)

APPLY

Think about travel under water. Write three sentences. Tell about it. Use an adverb in each sentence.

Review: Pronouns

A *pronoun* stands for one or more nouns.

One way to use a pronoun is in place of a subject noun.

Look at this example.

Americans like to play. **They** like games.

What subject pronoun replaced a noun?

Different pronouns are used in other parts of a sentence. What noun is replaced by the pronoun below?

Adults play games. Children play **them,** too.

You use the pronouns *I* and *me* to talk about yourself. Use *I* only in the subject. Use *me* in other parts of the sentence. When you talk about yourself and someone else, name yourself last.

Look at these sentences.

Tina and I played a game.
I thought the game was fun.
Tina told me that the game was hard.
Al invited Tina and me to play.

Find the subject in each sentence. Notice the use of *I* and *me.*

If you need more help with the Practice, look back at pages 186–193.

PRACTICE

A. (Written) Write the correct pronoun.

Example: In school (we/us) are learning about China.
we

1. Dad is taking (me/I) there some day.
2. He and (I/me) will go on a tour.
3. Chinese writing looks different to (we/us).
4. Instead of letters, (they/them) use picture words.
5. Most people do not learn all of (them/they).

B. (Written) Make two lists. Label one *Subject.* Label one *Other Sentence Parts.* Put the pronouns in the correct lists.

Example: We will go with them the next time.

Subject	Other Sentence Parts
We	**them**

6. Finally she threw it.
7. In the past, you brought them all.
8. Yesterday Kevin and I called her.
9. Tomorrow he will give you the book.
10. Yes, it is next to him.

APPLY

Write three sentences about a ball game. Use pronouns instead of nouns.

Editing a Paragraph

Writing a paragraph takes time. It does not end when the words are on paper. You must edit what you write. Make sure your writing is clear and correct.

Find the six mistakes in this paragraph.

Guide Dogs

Guide dogs they are trained to work with blind people. go to special schools. They learns to walk with the person. They learn to guide the person on the streets. Them are taught to take orders from the persin They are trained to avoid danger.

Review these Guidelines.

GUIDELINES

1. Start each sentence with a capital letter. End each with the correct punctuation mark.
2. Start each proper noun with a capital letter.
3. Check that each sentence has a subject and a predicate.
4. Make sure each verb matches its subject.
5. Use one form of an adjective to compare two things. Use another form for three things.
6. Check pronoun forms and spelling.

PRACTICE/APPLY

A. (Written) Edit this paragraph. It has five mistakes. Write the paragraph correctly on your paper.

Words come to we from many places. We eats crackers named for sylvester Graham. They are one of the most commonest of all foods. Named for the Earl of Sandwich.

B. (Written) Now edit this paragraph. It has four mistakes. Write the paragraph correctly on your paper.

Did you know that clear glass is made from sand The sand is melted and then shaped. is formed into glasses and windowes before it gets hard. Me can barely believe it was once part of a beach.

References

References are tools. They help you find information. You need to know what tool to use.

A *dictionary* tells about words. Use it to find the spelling of a word. It will have the meaning, too. Use it to learn how to say a word. A dictionary may tell if a word is a noun, verb, adjective, or adverb.

Use an *encyclopedia* to find out more about a subject or person.

Choose an *almanac* to find out about a certain year. An almanac lists many facts and figures.

Read *newspapers* for facts that change each day.

There are many other references. A *telephone directory* has addresses and phone numbers. *Maps* show where places are. *Calendars* tell you dates and days. *Cookbooks* show how to buy, cook, and store food.

PRACTICE

A. (Oral) For each question, tell if you would use a *dictionary,* an *encyclopedia,* or an *almanac.*

Example: Which spelling is correct, *neice* or *niece?*
dictionary

1. What do starfish eat?
2. How many cars were made in Detroit last year?
3. Where was George Washington born?
4. How do you say *bruise?*
5. How many planets are there?
6. Is *peace* a noun or a verb?
7. Who won the World Series last year?

B. (Written) For each question, write *map, telephone book, cookbook, calendar,* or *newspaper.*

Example: How do you cook corn?
cookbook

1. What time is the evening news on TV?
2. How long do you cook oatmeal?
3. Is Kansas City in Kansas?
4. On what day of the week is next July 4?
5. Who won yesterday's town election?
6. What is Sid Brown's address?
7. What lake lies between Vermont and New York?

APPLY

Make up three things that might be in an almanac in 1999. Write a sentence about each.

Notes

Notes help you remember what you read. When you take notes, write only the most important words. Do not write whole sentences.

How do you know which facts are important? Ask yourself WH-questions. They are *who, what, when, where, why,* and *how.* The answers will be your notes.

You may not be able to answer every question. Write the answers you do find.

Read this paragraph.

California has many schools. One is special. It is an acting school for animals. The school is Gentle Jungle in Colton. The teachers are animal trainers. They train animals you see in ads and movies. The animals are treated very well. They get food and love when they do what is asked. This is training by kindness.

What is the school? Where is it? Why are animals sent there? Who teaches them? How?

Your notes for the answers to the question *how* might look like this.

Training by kindness
Treat well
Food and love

PRACTICE

A. (Written) Write the headings *Who, What, When, Where, Why,* and *How.* Read the paragraph. Ask yourself WH-questions. Make notes. Write your answers under the correct headings.

In 1893 a famous song was written. Two sisters in New York wrote "Good Morning to You." The sisters were Mildred and Patty Hill. The song was not a big hit at first. Then the sisters changed it a little. The song quickly became a hit. Its new title was "Happy Birthday to You."

B. (Written) Write the headings *Who, What, When, Where, Why,* and *How.* Then read the paragraph. Ask yourself WH-questions. Write notes under the correct heading.

Paintings are not always done on paper. Some painters draw and paint on the walls of city buildings. These paintings are called murals. Some of them are very large. People like murals. They can see and enjoy them everyday.

APPLY

What was the last picture you drew or painted? Write three sentences about it.

Putting Notes in Order

Take notes to help you remember details. Write only the important details. Notes are of most use if they are in good *order*.

Notes are put in order easily. Think about what you read. Look for the main idea.

What is the main idea in this paragraph?

Many toys people now enjoy are not new. Some, such as balls and kites, have been the same for years. Chess and checkers have changed only a little. Chinese checkers is not Chinese.

The first sentence states the main idea. The next two add details. The last sentence is not needed. It tells nothing about the main idea.

Look at the order of these notes.

Many toys not new
Balls, kites—not changed
Chess, checkers—changed

An outline helps you put notes in order. The outline does not have complete sentences. Where is the main idea? The first word of the main idea begins with a capital letter. What are the details? Their first words start with capital letters, too.

PRACTICE

A. (Oral) Read each set of notes. They are not in order. Tell how the notes should be put in order.

1. Long rice good for fried rice
   Two kinds of rice
   Short rice good for porridge

2. Bean sprouts grown from beans
   Dried beans make noodles
   Many foods from beans

3. Plain ones from wood
   Many kinds of chopsticks
   Fancy ones from ivory

B. (Written) Read the paragraph. Write an outline. Start with the main idea. Note the details that tell about this idea.

   Harp seals are good swimmers. They are at home in icy waters. They twist and turn with ease. These seals can dive as deep as 600 feet. They can stay underwater for 30 minutes. They can swim long distances.

APPLY

Write three sentences that tell why taking notes is helpful.

Review: Irregular Verbs

> **Add *-ed* to most verbs to show past tense. Irregular verbs do not form the past tense with *-ed*.**

Verbs can show *time*. A verb that shows past time is in the *past tense*. You form the past tense of most verbs by adding *-ed*. For example, you change *jump* to *jumped* to show past time.

Remember that *irregular verbs* are different. They are changed in the past tense. You have learned about many irregular verbs.

Review the verbs in the chart.

Irregular Verbs

Present Tense→Past Tense			
know→knew	throw→threw	teach→taught	do→did
take→took	catch→caught	sit→sat	eat→ate
see→saw	come→came	think→thought	

The verbs *know* and *throw* are alike in one way. They are also alike in the past tense in one way. In what way are they alike? How are *teach* and *catch* alike?

If you need more help with the Practice, look back at pages 118–119, 234–235, and 246–249.

PRACTICE

A. (Written) Write the correct verb.

Example: Last year Mom (catch/caught) the biggest fish.
caught

1. Yesterday Angel (threw/throws) better than I.
2. Now Mrs. Baker (taught/teaches) math.
3. Now watch Grandma (threw/throw) it.
4. I (knew/know) that story when I was in first grade.
5. Martin (did/does) all his work yesterday.
6. Last week she (caught/catches) the last bus.

B. (Written) Write the correct verb for each sentence.

7. The magician (took/takes) one card now.
8. Now I (saw/see) what you mean!
9. Last year Harry (sat/sits) in front of me.
10. Becky (came/comes) a little late last time.
11. Bruce (thought/thinks) he can fix the clock now.
12. Yesterday Jaina (took/takes) all the books back.
13. They (ate/eat) a big breakfast yesterday.
14. You (came/come) now with Emily and me.

APPLY

Write three sentences about a meal you ate away from home. Use an irregular verb in each sentence.

Review: Contractions

> A *contraction* is a short way of writing two words. An apostrophe is used with it.

You can make *contractions* with pronouns and verbs. Drop a letter or letters. Put in an *apostrophe* ('). Always use an apostrophe. It shows where letters were dropped.

You know that many contractions are made with the verbs *be* and *have*. These may not always be in the present tense.

Look at these contractions.

> I'm   he's   they're   she'll
> he'd   you've   we'll   you'd

From what words were they made?

Contractions are formed using a verb and *not*.

What words were joined in these contractions?

> aren't   isn't   haven't   wasn't
> hasn't   didn't   doesn't   don't

Think about the contractions *can't* and *won't*. How are they different from the ones you read? Which contraction has two letters dropped? What word was changed to form the other contraction?

If you need more help with the Practice, look back at pages 202–203 and 250–251.

PRACTICE

A. (Written) Form contractions from the underlined words. Write the contractions.

> **Example:** <u>I will</u> write to you.
> **I'll**

1. <u>You are</u> reading words.
2. <u>They are</u> made from letters.
3. Here <u>it is</u> common to use the English alphabet.
4. <u>You would</u> enjoy seeing writing in Russian.
5. <u>They have</u> different letters.

B. (Written) Form contractions from the underlined words. Write the contractions.

6. Wait, you <u>are not</u> writing words.
7. Oh, that <u>is not</u> a word at all.
8. We <u>do not</u> use Roman numerals often.
9. The Romans <u>did not</u> use numerals like ours.
10. I <u>have not</u> seen all the Roman numerals.
11. Now I <u>cannot</u> remember what X stands for.
12. Thanks, I <u>will not</u> forget that it means "ten."

APPLY

Write three sentences. Tell what you think might be different in another place. Use contractions.

Review: Correcting Sentences

> A *sentence* is a group of words telling a complete thought. Sentences that run on and on should be made into shorter sentences.

Some groups of words tell only part of a thought. They are not sentences.

Look at these groups of words.

    is big. Ghost towns

Something is missing. *What* is big?
What *about* ghost towns?

Look how each thought is completed here.

    The city is big. Ghost towns **are empty.**

Some sentences run on and on. Capital letters are missing. There is no end punctuation. These sentences can be fixed. The example shows how.

    Incorrect: Some places are quite hot it is hard to live in a desert usually few people live there.

    Correct: Some places are quite hot. It is hard to live in a desert. Usually few people live there.

If you need more help with the Practice, look back at pages 10–17.

PRACTICE

A. (Written) There are six incomplete sentences. Turn each into a sentence. Write correct sentences.

   Most people eat local foods. get easily. For example, Japan is an island country. four big islands. water on all sides. many fish. The Japanese eat a lot of fish. It is moist in Japan. can grow rice. eat much rice, too.

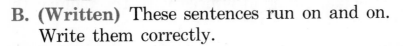

B. (Written) These sentences run on and on. Write them correctly.

1. Many Japanese homes have soft floor mats visitors do not wear shoes inside they take them off first.
2. Some eating places hang menus outside people can see what they want before they go in.
3. Many people eat with chopsticks you can eat with one hand eating with a knife and fork takes two hands.

APPLY

   What foods do you think people in this country eat often? Write three sentences telling what the foods are. Be sure to write complete thoughts.

Review: Correcting Sentences

> A *sentence* has a subject and a predicate. The verb in the predicate should match the subject.

A subject can be a noun or a pronoun. *I, she, he,* and *it* are singular pronouns.

Look at these sentences.

> He pulls off the hat.
> I look at his curly hair.

Which singular pronoun is used with the plain verb form?

Use the plain verb form with plural subjects. Plural subjects may be nouns or pronouns. Plural nouns mean *we, you,* or *they.* Plural pronouns are *we, you,* and *they.* You do not use the *s*-form with plural subjects.

Look for negative words. Do not use two in one sentence. Remember that contractions can be negative, too. Use either a negative word or a negative contraction.

Look at these examples. Both are correct.

> My hair **doesn't** have any curls.
> My hair has **no** curls.

If you need more help with the Practice, look back at pages 114–117, 228–233, and 252–253.

PRACTICE

A. (Written) Complete each sentence.

> **Example:** Hair (grow/grows) on your head.
> **grows**

1. Juan (has/have) dark hair.
2. My brothers (has/have) red hair.
3. It (is/are) keeping his head warm.
4. You (see/sees) hair on faces, too.
5. For example, eyelashes (protect/protects) your eyes.
6. Hair in your nose (keep/keeps) dust out.

B. (Written) Complete each sentence.

> **Example:** Jess won't call (anybody/nobody).
> **anybody**

7. Sally isn't going (anywhere/nowhere).
8. I don't (never/ever) want to find out!
9. The children had (nothing/anything) to do.
10. In winter the birds did not have (no/any) nests.
11. Now no one (will/won't) get hurt.
12. Until now Chris (never/ever) tried very hard.

APPLY

Write three health or safety rules. At least one should tell people something they should not do.

15

Reports

You know an author can make up a story. A story may be true. It may tell about things that are not real. Reports are different. *Reports* tell about things that are real. They may tell about real people. They may tell about real events.

Look at this report.

A Special Seal

Andre is a special seal. He lives in Rockport, Maine. He belongs to a man named Harry. Andre does tricks with Harry. People travel a long way to see Andre do his tricks.

What is this report about? The first sentence tells what Andre is. What do the others tell? They give more facts about Andre.

The first sentence is the topic sentence. It tells what the paragraph is about. The other sentences tell more about the topic. They add details.

Look at the first line of the report. How is it different from the other lines? It is indented. The first line of every paragraph starts this way. Then you know when a new paragraph begins.

PRACTICE

A. (Written) Write a paragraph with these sentences. Put the topic sentence first.

> They swim very well, but they do not fly.
> Penguins are black and white birds.
> They live only near the South Pole.

B. (Written) Write a paragraph with these sentences. Put the topic sentence first. Leave out any sentence that is not about the topic.

> Doorknobs are also round.
> A phone dial is round.
> The phone is helpful.
> Many things are round.

APPLY

Write three sentences about round shapes you see at home. Begin with a topic sentence.

16

Topics

Suppose you want to write a report. The first thing to do is decide on a topic. The *topic* is what the report is about. If you had a pet bird named JB, you might write about it.

"JB's green feathers" would not be a good topic to write about. It is too small a topic. How many details could you write about?

"Pet birds of the world" is not a good topic, either. It is too big. There are too many details to write in a short report.

A good topic might be "my bird JB." There would be many things you could tell about JB.

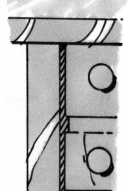

Now you have a topic. You can start your report. First write a topic sentence. The topic sentence tells what the topic is.

Here is a good topic sentence.

I have a funny bird named JB.

There are probably many funny things about JB. These things are the details. What other topic sentences could you write about JB?

PRACTICE

A. (Oral) Here are some topic sentences for a report. The report is on bluebirds. It tells about their population problem. Name the topic sentence that best fits the topic.

> There are not many bluebirds anymore.
> Bluebirds have blue backs and orange chests.
> Many birds live in birdhouses.
> Bluebirds live in open fields.
> Blackbirds are large, noisy birds.

B. (Written) Here is a list of topics. They are all too big. Pick one topic. Make it smaller so it is a good topic for a short report.

> farms of the world
> the history of cats
> how to cook everything

APPLY

Think of a topic to write a report about. Write a good topic sentence for it.

A Report: Plan, Write, Edit

A *report* tells the facts about something. The *topic sentence* tells what the report is about. Other sentences tell *details* about the topic.

PLAN

Look at the picture. What big event is taking place? Be a reporter. Write a report about it.

Write the headings *Who, What, When,* and *Where.* Write one detail for each heading. Find details in the picture.

WRITE

Use the plan and write your report. Do not forget to indent the first line of a paragraph. Can you think of a good title?

Use the Guidelines for help.

GUIDELINES

1. Write the report title correctly. The first, last, and all other important words begin with capitals.
2. The topic sentence is usually the first sentence.
3. The details come after the topic sentence.

EDIT

Now you have written your report. You are ready to edit it. Practice editing on this report. Correct the seven mistakes.

A Great Magician

He made rabbits pop out of hats? Harry Houdini he were a great magician. He could escape from locked boxs. He could undo locked chains. He once tries to make an elephant disappear. Houdini died on Halloween in 1926.

Now edit your report. Use the Guidelines.

GUIDELINES

1. Write the title correctly.
2. Indent the first line of the paragraph.
3. Check for a topic sentence.
4. Include interesting details. Check that they are in order.
5. Make sure nouns and verbs agree.
6. Use the right form for verbs. Check spelling.

Is your report correct now? Does it tell about what is happening? Copy your report in your best handwriting.

An Oral Report

Do not be afraid to give a report! You know how to tell a story. A report is like a story. You should be prepared for your report.

Use these Guidelines.

GUIDELINES

1. Think of what your listeners would be interested in knowing.
2. Make notes on what you want to say.
3. Look at your notes before you start.
4. Tell the report in the correct order.
5. Speak loudly and clearly. Do not speak too fast.
6. Look at your listeners while you speak.

Learn to be a good listener, too. Watch the person giving the report. Be polite. Do not talk during the report. Think about what is being said. Wait until the report is over to ask questions.

PRACTICE/APPLY

(Oral) Give a report to the class. Use the facts from the report you wrote for Lesson 17. You may tell about something else you know about.

Keep Practicing

A. Matching Subjects and Verbs
Write the correct verb for each sentence. *(Unit 6, Lesson 1)*

1. This morning Ed (is/am) drawing.
2. Ed (use/uses) a red crayon to draw sea horses.
3. Then the drawings (is/are) covered with paint.
4. The paint (stick/sticks) only to the paper.
5. Wax crayon marks do not (get/gets) covered.

Write the correct verb for each sentence. *(Unit 6, Lesson 2)*

6. He (make) a fingerprint drawing.
7. First I (press) my finger on a pad with ink on it.
8. Next she (roll) my finger on paper.
9. Now they (draw) little feet and a head on the print.
10. See, it (look) like a turtle.

B. Using *Has* and *Have*
Use *has* or *have* to finish each sentence. *(Unit 6, Lesson 3)*

1. Milk (have/has) different uses.
2. We (have/has) cheese made from ours.
3. You (have/has) some cottage cheese, too.
4. Of course, Sara (have/has) other cheeses.
5. I (have/has) cheddar cheese.
6. This sandwich (has/have) cheese in it.
7. Maria (has/have) cheese and apple slices.

C. Helping Verbs

Write the complete verbs. Circle the helping verbs. *(Unit 6, Lesson 4)*

1. I am making musical glasses.
2. He has filled six glasses with water.
3. He was filling one halfway.
4. Tom has left that one almost empty.
5. Now he is tapping each glass with a spoon.
6. Each one is making a different sound.
7. Ginger and Tom have tapped all the glasses.
8. We have played a little tune!
9. For years I have loved glass music.

D. Irregular Verbs

Write the correct verb for each sentence. *(Unit 6, Lessons 5, 10, and 11)*

1. Last night Steve (ate/eat) two hamburgers.
2. They (sit/sat) at the station all yesterday.
3. Now Mary (thought/thinks) we can go.
4. Now Nellie (ate/eats) cheese and crackers, too.
5. You (took/take) the bus last week.
6. Pepper (did/does) two tricks now.
7. Yesterday I (thought/think) it was a lovely day.
8. Sandy and Peter (sit/sat) by the window now.
9. I (came/come) on the same bus now.
10. Last week Fran (saw/sees) you at the zoo.

E. Contractions with *Not*
Write contractions for the underlined words.
(Unit 6, Lesson 12)

1. This family <u>does not</u> waste energy.
2. Mark <u>will not</u> keep the water running.
3. Also, the twins <u>have not</u> forgotten.
4. They <u>do not</u> leave the freezer door open long.
5. Mom and Dad <u>are not</u> always using the dryer.
6. They <u>did not</u> keep as many lights on, either.
7. They <u>have not</u> watered the grass a lot.
8. They <u>will not</u> forget to save energy.
9. Energy <u>does not</u> save itself.

F. Avoiding Double Negatives
Write the correct word to complete each
sentence. *(Unit 6, Lesson 13)*

1. Now Barbara hasn't (<u>no/any</u>) pencils.
2. After lunch, nobody said (<u>nothing/anything</u>).
3. Sorry, there aren't (<u>any/none</u>) left.
4. Lisa won't (<u>ever/never</u>) lose the key.
5. You and Chan Wong have made (<u>no/any</u>) mistakes.
6. My sandals aren't (<u>nowhere/anywhere</u>)!
7. That brook will (<u>never/ever</u>) run dry.
8. No one brought (<u>nothing/anything</u>) to eat.
9. No one can do (<u>anything/nothing</u>) about it.
10. I haven't (<u>no/any</u>) money.

G. Punctuating Conversations

Each sentence has one mistake. Write each sentence correctly. *(Unit 6, Lesson 7)*

1. Tony called, "Where is everyone"
2. "That bread is delicious, said Susan.
3. Morris said "I really enjoyed myself."
4. Rosa replied, "we can go now."
5. Lou asked, "Whose shoe is this?
6. Everything shines, said Janet.
7. Mako answered, "they are waiting."
8. Julia shouted, "Let's race"

H. Causes

Write *C* if the second sentence in each pair was caused by the first. Write *X* if there is no cause for the action. *(Unit 6, Lesson 9)*

1. Glenn stayed up too late. He is tired today.
2. My shoelace broke. I bought a new one.
3. The sun is bright. Scott is catching a cold.
4. The door was left open. The room is cold now.
5. Sally got caught in the rain. She is wet.
6. Our picnic is finished. The car is red.
7. Pat dropped the cup. The cup broke.
8. The book is heavy. Today is Thursday.
9. Eric hit the switch. The light went out.
10. Carla told a funny story. Everyone laughed.

Something Extra

Good References

One word can have more than one meaning. A dictionary lists the different meanings of a word. It also shows how to use a word in a sentence. Read the dictionary entries for *hog* and *bar*.

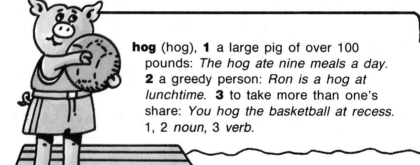

hog (hog), **1** a large pig of over 100 pounds: *The hog ate nine meals a day.* **2** a greedy person: *Ron is a hog at lunchtime.* **3** to take more than one's share: *You hog the basketball at recess.* 1, 2 *noun*, 3 *verb*.

bar (bar), **1** a straight piece of wood or iron: *The thief was behind prison bars.* **2** a rectangle of something: *Gwen bought a bar of soap.* **3** the profession of law: *You have to pass a bar exam to become a lawyer.* **4** an underwater bank of sand or dirt: *The boat was stuck on a bar of sand.* **5** the up-and-down lines on music paper: *The sheet music had many music bars on it.* *noun*.

Find the Word

Now complete each sentence below. Use clues from the dictionary entry for *bar*. Write the missing words.

1. "I feel like I am behind ＿＿ bars in this pen," said Harry Hog.
2. "Who erased the ＿＿ bars from my music sheet?" snorted Hilda Hog.
3. "Help me get my boat off this bar of ＿＿!" shouted Mel Hog.
4. "Pass the bar of ＿＿," said the cleanest hog in the pen.
5. "Have you passed the bar ＿＿ yet?" asked lawyer Larry Hog.

Solve this riddle. Use the first letters from the answers above.

What did one hog say to the other hog?

Don't ＿2＿ ＿5＿ ＿3＿ ＿4＿ with ＿2＿ ＿5＿ !

Don't mess with me!

Handbook

GRAMMAR/USAGE

SENTENCES

A **sentence** is a group of words telling a whole thought. (page 10)

> An elephant lives long.

A **statement** tells something. A **question** asks something. An **exclamation** tells something with strong feeling. (page 12)

> A whale is not a fish.   Where do whales live?
> The whale is huge!

A **Yes-No question** asks for a yes or no answer. (page 32)

> Is Pete going to the circus? Yes.

WH-questions begin with *who, what, when, where, why,* and *how.* (page 34)

> <u>Who</u> went to the zoo?   <u>How</u> do whales sing?

Every sentence has a subject. The **subject** tells whom or what the sentence is about. (page 28)

> <u>Whales</u>|swim fast.

Every sentence has a predicate. The **predicate** tells what the subject does, is, or has. (page 30)

> Whales|<u>travel</u>.   Whales|<u>are sea animals.</u>

Subjects and verbs must match. (pages 116, 228, 230, 232)

> A <u>lion eats</u> meat.   <u>Lions hunt</u> large animals.

A **helping verb** must match its subject. (page 238)

> A robin <u>is</u> singing.   We <u>have</u> finished.

PARTS OF SPEECH

Nouns

A **noun** is a word that names any person, place, or thing. A noun may be **singular** or **plural.** (pages 52, 54, 56)

girl→girls   beach→beaches   berry→berries

A **common noun** names any person, place, or thing. A **proper noun** names a special person, place, or thing. (pages 58, 60)

boy→Bill Jones   street→Elm Street   day→Monday

A **possessive noun** is a noun that shows who or what owns or has something. A singular or plural noun can be changed to show possession. (pages 74, 76)

Singular: an anteater's tongue
Plural: the chickens' eggs, the children's books

The words *a, an,* and *the* are **articles.** They mark nouns. Use *a* or *an* with a singular noun. Use *an* before a word that begins with a vowel. Use *the* with all nouns. (page 72)

a pear   an orange   the pear   the pears

Pronouns

A **pronoun** stands for one or more nouns. A **subject pronoun** takes the place of a subject noun. (pages 186, 192)

Roy baked a cake.   He baked a cake.

Other pronouns take the place of nouns in other parts of sentences. (pages 188, 192)

Dad blew the candles out.   He blew them out.

Subject Pronouns
I
you
he, she, it
we
you
they

Other Pronouns
me
you
him, her, it
us
you
them

Verbs

A **verb** is always in the predicate part of a sentence. An **action verb** shows what someone or something does. (page 98)

The robin|<u>sings</u> a happy song.

Some verbs do not show action. They tell what someone or something is, was, or will be. (page 99)

The clown <u>is</u> happy.   The clown <u>was</u> sad.

A verb that names an action happening now is in the **present tense.** (page 100)

Snowflakes <u>fall</u> from the clouds.

A **past tense** verb tells about the past. (pages 102, 118)

Yesterday Kate <u>played</u> baseball.

A verb that tells about the future is in the **future tense.** (page 104)

Tomorrow Sid <u>will finish</u> his plane.

The present tenses of the verbs **be, have,** and **do** have different forms. (pages 114, 232, 248)

<u>be</u>: I am, you are, he/she/it is, we/you/they are
<u>have</u>: I have, you have, he/she/it has, we/you/they
  have
<u>do</u>: I do, you do, he/she/it does, we/you/they do

A **helping verb** is a verb that goes with a main verb. (page 233)

I <u>am</u> going to Houston.   We <u>have</u> packed already.

The verbs **be** and **have** may be used as main verbs or helping verbs. (page 233)

I <u>am</u> sleepy. I <u>have tried</u> to train it.

Helping Verbs	
am	is
are	was
were	will
would	has
have	had

Irregular Verbs

Present	Past	Past with helping verb
am/is/are	was/were	been
catch	caught	caught
come	came	come
do/does	did	done
eat	ate	eaten
have/has	had	had
know	knew	known
see	saw	seen
sit	sat	sat
take	took	taken
teach	taught	taught
throw	threw	thrown

Adjectives

An **adjective** is a word that tells about a noun. It may tell color, size, or shape. It may tell about what you see, hear, feel, smell, or taste. (pages 140, 142)

green mountains small lake round ball
salty crackers loud thunder hard chair

An adjective can be changed to show how one thing compares with another. When you compare two things, use the ending **-er.** Also use the word *than.* (page 144)

A whale is larger than an elephant.

When you compare three or more things, use the **-est** ending. (page 144)

> The whale is the <u>largest</u> animal of all.

Do not add *-er* or *-est* to long adjectives. Use **more** and **most.** (page 146)

> comfortable   more comfortable   most comfortable

Adverbs

An **adverb** tells more about a verb. (page 158)

> An iceberg melts <u>slowly</u>.

An adverb may answer the question **where, when,** or **how.** (pages 158, 160, 162)

> An iceberg floated <u>nearby</u>.   <u>Yesterday</u> we saw it.

Many adverbs end in **-ly.** Some adjectives can be changed to adverbs by adding **-ly.** (page 164)

> bright + -ly = brightly   clever + -ly = cleverly

USAGE PROBLEMS

Not every group of words is a sentence. A sentence must tell a whole thought. (page 10)

> <u>Not a sentence</u>: live in a glass tank
> <u>Sentence</u>: Some fish live in a glass tank.

Sentences should not run together. (page 16)

> <u>Incorrect</u>: The fish live in a tank it is large.
> <u>Correct</u>: The fish live in a tank. It is large.
> <u>Incorrect</u>: We went to Sea World and we saw
>   many sea animals and we enjoyed the visit.
> <u>Correct</u>: We went to Sea World. We saw many sea
>   animals. We enjoyed the visit.

When you talk about yourself and someone else, name yourself last. Use **I** in the subject part of a sentence. Use **me** in the other part. (page 190)

Ana and I are friends. Bob sees Ana and me.

Two sentences may repeat the same noun. It may be better to use a pronoun in the second sentence. (page 204)

The plane flew to Dallas. ~~The plane~~ It landed there.

When you use a subject pronoun, be sure to drop the subject noun or nouns. (page 206)

Incorrect: Dan he took the bus.
Correct: Dan took the bus. Or: He took the bus.

Do not use two **negative words** in the same sentence. (page 252)

Incorrect: I don't have no pen.
Correct: I don't have a pen. Or: I have no pen.

CAPITALIZATION

A **sentence** begins with a capital letter. (pages 10, 14)

He found five tadpoles.

A **proper noun** begins with a capital letter. (pages 58, 60)

Ben Franklin   Main Street   New York City

An **abbreviation** starts with a capital letter if the word it stands for starts with one. (page 66)

Mrs. Lund   Wed.   Mar.   Market St.   Fla.

The first word in the **greeting** and in the **closing** of a letter begins with a capital letter. (pages 70, 122, 126)

Dear Julia, Yours truly,

The first word of a **quotation** begins with a capital letter. (page 240)

Anna shouted, "Look at the rocket!"

The first, the last, and all the important words in a **title** begin with capital letters. (page 258)

The Adventures of the Wind and the Sun

PUNCTUATION

End Punctuation

A **statement** ends with a **period.** (pages 10, 12, 14)

Whales dive under the water.

Most **abbreviations** end with a **period.** (pages 66, 67)

Mrs. Thurs. Apr. St. Tex.

A **question** ends with a **question mark (?).** (pages 12, 14)

Will we see the whales?

An **exclamation** ends with an **exclamation mark (!).** (pages 12, 14)

I love parades! Watch that whale!

Comma

Use a comma **(,)** with **dates.** Put the comma between the day and the year. (page 68)

April 23, 1929 July 4, 1983

Use a comma in a **list** of three or more words in a sentence. (page 68)
Martha and Luis eat pears, apples, and grapes.

Use a comma between a **city** and **state**. (page 70)
Boston, MA   Sitka, Alaska

Use a comma after the **greeting** in a friendly letter and after the letter **closing**. (page 70)
Dear Alice,   Dear Uncle Jim,   Sincerely,

Use a comma when the **speaker tag** comes before the speaker's words in a quotation. (page 240)
Pablo asked, "Who is on the phone?"

Colon
Use a colon (**:**) after the **greeting** in a business letter. (page 122)
Dear Mr. Allen: Dear Miss Lopez:

Apostrophe
Use an apostrophe (**'**) to form singular or plural **possessive nouns.** (pages 74, 76)
Singular: a snake's eyes   Plural: the lions' roar

Use an apostrophe with a **contraction.** (pages 202, 250)
he is→he's   they would→they'd   cannot→can't

Quotation Marks
Use quotation marks (**" "**) around a speaker's words in a **quotation.** Use a punctuation mark (**!?,**) between the quotation and speaker tag. (page 240)
"What are you wearing to the party?" Jean asked.

SPELLING

Plurals

To make many nouns plural, just add **-s.** (page 54)
> home→homes window→windows

To make nouns that end in *ch, sh, ss, s, x,* or *zz*
plural, add **-es.** (pages 54, 56)
> dish→dishes bus→buses fox→foxes

To make nouns that end with a consonant and *y*
plural, change the *y* to *i* and add **-es.** (page 56)
> lady→ladies city→cities

A few nouns must be changed in other ways. (page
56)
> foot→feet mouse→mice child→children

Possessive Nouns

To form the possessive of most singular nouns, add
's. (page 74)
> the duck's bill an elephant's trunk

To form the possessive of plural nouns that end
with *s,* add only an apostrophe (**'**). (page 76)
> the tigers' stripes the lions' manes

To form the possessive of plural nouns that do not
end with *s,* add **'s.** (page 76)
> the children's hair the women's hands

Verbs

To make the *s*-form of verbs, add **-s.** (page 100)
> look→looks clap→claps

To make the *s*-form of verbs that end with *ch, sh, ss, s, x,* or *zz,* add **-es.** (page 100)

 catch→catches tax→taxes buzz→buzzes

To make the *s*-form of a verb that ends with a consonant letter and *y,* change *y* to *i* and add **-es.** (page 100)

 spy→spies worry→worries

To form the past tense of most verbs, add **-ed.** (page 102)

 repeat→repeated answer→answered

To form the past tense of a verb that ends with a final *e,* drop the *e.* (page 102)

 cause→caused handle→handled

To form the past tense of a verb that ends with a single letter vowel followed by a single final consonant, double the consonant. (page 102)

 plan→planned shop→shopped

To make the past tense of a verb ending with a consonant letter and *y,* change *y* to *i.* (page 102)

 empty→emptied hurry→hurried

The past tenses of irregular verbs change spelling. (See Handbook page 320.)

Adding *-er* and *-est*

Add *-er* or *-est* to many **adjectives** to compare things. (page 144)

 shiny + -er = shinier (change *y* to *i*)
 fine + -er = finer (drop *e*)
 sad + -er = sadder (double final consonant)

Contractions

A contraction is a short way of writing two words. An **apostrophe (')** is always used to show where letters are dropped. (pages 202, 250)

> it is→it's   they are→they're   cannot→can't

VOCABULARY

Synonyms are words that have almost the same meaning. (page 154)

> noisy—loud   unhappy—sad

Antonyms are words that have almost opposite meanings. (page 155)

> strong—weak   top—bottom

A **prefix** is a word part. It is added to the beginning of a word. It changes the word's meaning. (page 156)

> un- + pack = unpack   re- + shape = reshape

WRITING

The Steps

Plan: When you plan something to write, you decide *what* you want to say and *to whom.*

✔ Think about the people who are going to read what you write. Think about what they would need to know.

✔ Make notes about the main points you want to cover. Make notes about details.

✔ Check all your facts.

Write: When you write something, you try to say what you mean as clearly as possible.

✔ Remember any special Guidelines or Reminders for the kind of writing you are doing.

✔ Use your planning notes to write complete sentences.

✔ Be sure your sentences say what you want to say.

✔ Put your sentences in an order that makes sense.

Edit: When you edit something, you look for any problems that might keep your reader from understanding what you are trying to say.

✔ Read what you wrote. Make sure it says what you want it to say. Is it in an order that makes sense?

✔ Check for mistakes in grammar.

✔ Check for mistakes in punctuation or spelling.

✔ Copy your edited work in your neatest handwriting.

Some Forms

Paragraph (pages 40, 42, 172)

What a cluttered place the hobby shop is! Red, blue, silver, and yellow planes swing from the ceiling. On the right, dozens of ships with white sails are on the long counter. Big and small kites hang on the back wall. Trains roar and whistle around a large table in the middle of the floor. The counter on the left is piled with soft rugs.

Invitation (page 84)

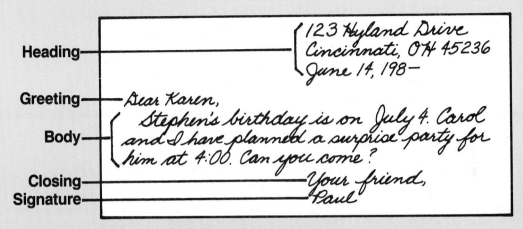

Heading
> 123 Hyland Drive
> Cincinnati, OH 45236
> June 14, 198—

Greeting
Dear Karen,

Body
> Stephen's birthday is on July 4. Carol and I have planned a surprise party for him at 4:00. Can you come?

Closing
Your friend,

Signature
Paul

Business Letter (page 124)

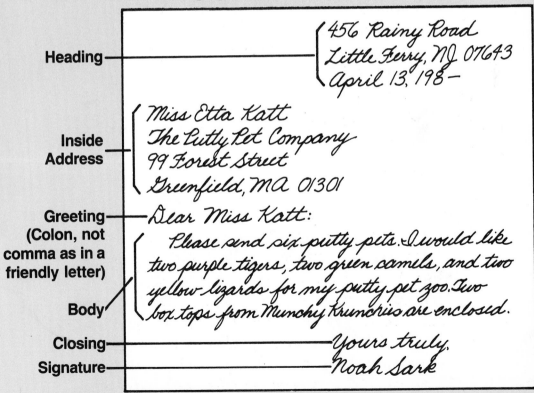

Heading
> 456 Rainy Road
> Little Ferry, NJ 07643
> April 13, 198—

Inside Address
> Miss Etta Katt
> The Putty Pet Company
> 99 Forest Street
> Greenfield, MA 01301

Greeting (Colon, not comma as in a friendly letter)
Dear Miss Katt:

Body
> Please send six putty pets. I would like two purple tigers, two green camels, and two yellow lizards for my putty pet zoo. Two box tops from Munchy Krunchies are enclosed.

Closing
Yours truly,

Signature
Noah Sark

Envelope (page 127)

Sender's Address — Noah Sark
456 Rainy Road
Little Ferry, NJ 07643

Receiver's Address — Miss Etta Katt
Putty Pet Company
99 Forest Street
Greenfield, MA 01301

LISTENING / SPEAKING

Listening
1. Sit quietly.
2. Look at the speaker.
3. Listen for the topic sentence.
4. Listen for details.
5. Do not interrupt.
6. Save your questions for the end.

Speaking
1. Think of what your listeners would be interested in hearing.
2. Make sure your topic is not too big.
3. Plan your speech, report, or story carefully.
4. Make notes to help you remember.
5. Look at your notes before you start.
6. Tell the story, speech, or report in correct order.
7. Look at the listeners while you speak.
8. Speak loudly and clearly.
9. Do not speak too fast.

More Practice

Sentences (pages 10–11)
   Two groups of words are sentences. Two are not.
Write the sentences.

1. A tiger is the biggest cat.
2. likes shade It
3. Tigers swim.
4. have black They stripes

   In the groups of words above that are not
sentences, put the words in an order that makes
sense.

> **Example:** People   books   read
> **People read books.**

Beginning and Ending Sentences (pages 12–13, 14–15)
   Number your paper from *1* to *7*. Correct each
sentence. Some sentences need a capital letter.
Some sentences need punctuation marks. Write *S*
if the sentence is a statement. Write *Q* if the
sentence is a question. Write *E* if the sentence is
an exclamation.

1. What happens to old paper money
2. a machine chops it.
3. the machine cuts the money up.
4. The government owns the machine
5. The government sells the tiny pieces
6. Do you have any old money
7. give it to me!

Correcting Sentences (pages 16–17)
   Write these sentences correctly. Add capital letters and periods.

1. The sponge is strange and this animal does not have a head and it does not have a heart or a stomach.
2. Sponges live on the ocean floor and they don't move and divers pick them.
3. People buy sponges they use them as cleaning tools.

Subjects and Predicates (pages 28–29, 30–31)
   Write these sentences. Underline the subject once. Underline the predicate twice.

1. Bones give you shape.
2. Your skeleton is made up of 206 bones.
3. You have 64 bones in just your two hands and arms.
4. Your backbone is made of up of 34 bones.
5. Bones grow like every other part of your body.

Yes-No and WH-Questions (pages 32–33, 34–35)
   Number your paper from *1* to *4*. Read these sentences. Find the two Yes-No questions. Write *Yes-No* next to their numbers.

1. Did you visit the Grand Canyon?
2. Who went with you?
3. What did you do at the Grand Canyon?
4. Did you send me a postcard?

Write the two WH-words in the remaining questions.

Writing: A Paragraph (pages 42–44)

Find a picture you like in a magazine. Then plan, write, and edit a paragraph about the picture. Write your main idea in an interesting topic sentence. Make sure your details tell about it. Use the Guidelines on page 44 to edit your paragraph.

Nouns (pages 52–53)

Number your paper from *1* to *7*. Write the nouns in each sentence.

1. Sometimes people talk to their plants.
2. Some men and women sing to their plants.
3. You and your friends can try out this idea.
4. Plant a small garden in the classroom.
5. The class can talk to one plant.
6. Do not talk to the other plant.
7. Watch to see how the plants grow.

Plural Nouns (pages 54–57)

Number your paper from *1* to *12.* Write the plural of each word.

1. class
2. flower
3. hatch
4. spy
5. cage
6. child
7. woman
8. branch
9. eye
10. party
11. box
12. berry

Proper Nouns (pages 58–59, 60–61)
Write a proper noun for each common noun. Use capitals correctly.

1. city   **2.** brother   **3.** day   **4.** month

Abbreviations (pages 66–67)
Write the abbreviations for these words.

1. January   **2.** Road   **3.** Monday   **4.** Street

Using Commas (pages 68–69)
Write each date correctly. Use commas and capital letters where they are needed.

1. August 17 1907   **2.** december 7 1941   **3.** october 6 1917

Write each sentence. Put commas where they belong.

1. Jane's socks were red green and white.
2. The names of the rabbits are Floppsy Mopsy and Peter.
3. The afternoon was warm wet and windy.

Capitals and Commas in Letters (pages 70–71)
Write each heading correctly. Use capital letters and commas where needed.

1. 123 brown avenue
Crockett, texas 75835
May 1 1982

2. 77 orchid road
hilo, hawaii 96720
November 4, 1979

Write each letter greeting and closing correctly.

1. dear sally   **3.** your friend   **4.** your cousin
2. dear ted   bruce   lulu

Using *A, An,* and *The* (pages 72–73)

Number your paper from *1* to *4.* Write the articles and the nouns they mark.

1. An automobile raced down the street.
2. The driver was a woman.
3. The car had a cage on the roof.
4. An eagle sat in the cage.

Number your paper from *1* to *5.* Read each sentence. Write the correct article.

1. Carl eats (a/an) apple every day.
2. Each morning Jan has (a/an) banana.
3. (A/The) grapes taste very sweet.
4. Marge likes (a/an) egg in (a/an) salad.
5. (A/The) beans look good in (a/the) salads.

Possessive Nouns (pages 74–75, 76–77)

Number your paper from *1* to *6.* Use fewer words. Write the possessive nouns with ' or 's.

1. the pet of my friend   **4.** the wings of a bird
2. the work of the boys   **5.** the names of the girls
3. the roar of the lions   **6.** the cars the men own

Number your paper from *1* to *6*. Write the possessive noun. Write *S* if the possessive noun is singular. Write *P* if it is plural.

1. Alex hunted for the children's toys.
2. My aunt's garden needs to be weeded.
3. The turtles' eggs warmed in the sun.
4. Jack's beanstalk just grows and grows.
5. The clowns' shoes squeak.
6. The birds' wings seem very short.

Writing: An Invitation (pages 84–86)

Invite a friend to a party or a picnic. Plan, write, and edit the invitation. Be sure to include the heading, the greeting, the body, and the closing. Answer the WH-questions. Remember to sign your name at the bottom. Use the Edit steps on page 86 to help you edit.

Verb Tenses (pages 100–101, 102–103, 104–105)

Write these sentences. Use the tense of the verb in parentheses at the end of each sentence.

Example: I *watched* (watch) a bee today. *past*

1. One bee ＿＿＿ (leave) the hive. *present*
2. It ＿＿＿ (move) from flower to flower. *present*
3. The bee ＿＿＿ (stop) in the patch of clover. *past*
4. It ＿＿＿ (collect) pollen. *future*
5. The bee ＿＿＿ (carry) the pollen on its legs. *present*

Using *Am, Is,* and *Are* (pages 114–115)
Write the correct verb for each sentence.

1. I (am/are) with my friends.
2. We (is/are) at the zoo.
3. The zoo (is/are) huge.
4. Many animals (is/are) here.
5. One building (is/are) full of birds.
6. The elephants (is/are) over there.
7. The tigers (is/are) here.
8. They (is/are) in cages.
9. Now they (is/are) behind a wall.

Matching Subjects and Verbs (pages 116–117)
Write the subject and verb in each sentence.
Underline plural subjects twice.

1. Spook Hill is a strange road in Florida.
2. Cars roll uphill on Spook Hill.
3. Water flows uphill, too.
4. A ball rolls up this strange road.
5. People are curious about Spook Hill.

Number your paper from *1* to *7.* Write the correct verb for each sentence beside the number.

1. A woman scientist (live/lives) in Africa.
2. She (study/studies) chimpanzees there.
3. The chimpanzees (climb/climbs) trees.
4. They (walk/walks) on the ground.

5. Sometimes the chimpanzees (act/acts) funny.

6. Her husband (work/works) with her.

7. He (help/helps) her in many ways.

Irregular Verbs (pages 118–119)

Write the correct past tense of these verbs.

1. catch   **3.** know

2. throw   **4.** teach

Write the verbs in these sentences. Underline the verbs in the past tense.

1. The monkey catches the banana.

2. It caught the banana easily.

3. Who threw it to the monkey?

4. Wendy throws the banana today.

5. We know the monkey's name.

Writing: A Business Letter (pages 124–126)

Plan, write, and edit a business letter. Choose a topic. (Example: Send to an airline for facts about trips to Hawaii.) Include a heading. Make up the name and an address for the inside address. In the body, say what you want. Tell where to send the item or information you want. Answer WH-questions. Include the six letter parts. Edit your letter. See the Guidelines on page 126. Then copy the letter in your best handwriting.

Adjectives (pages 140–141, 142–143)

Each sentence has an adjective that tells about one sense. Write the adjective.

1. The white car zoomed around the corner.
2. The warm sun melted the ice.
3. We listened to the loud crash of the waves.
4. Don't you like the salty smell of the ocean?
5. Ned ate all of the spicy meatballs.
6. The squeaky sound scared the puppy.
7. Puffy clouds rushed across the sky.

Using Adjectives That Compare (pages 144–145, 146–147)

Copy the three headings on your paper. Write each adjective. Then add the -er and the -est ending to each.

Adjective	**-er**	**-est**	
1. squeaky	3. strange	5. bright	7. thin
2. sad	4. flat	6. cloudy	8. happy

Rewrite each sentence so that it is correct.

1. The music is most enjoyable than the speech.
2. Nick's sled was the more unusual sled on the block.
3. Sunday is my more favorite day of the week.
4. She became a most famous singer than her brother.
5. Cathy painted a most remarkable picture than Sam.

Adverbs That Tell Where (pages 158–159)
   Write the adverbs that tell where.

1. We watch the whales outside of our submarine.
2. The whales swim around.
3. They dive down.
4. Two divers study the whales nearby.

Adverbs That Tell When (pages 160–161)
   Write the adverbs that tell when.

1. Today we are making a geography book.
2. We will begin early.
3. First we list the continents.
4. Then we tell about the oceans.

Adverbs That Tell How (pages 162–163)
   Write the adverbs that tell how.

1. Soldiers in red coats bravely guard the castle.
2. The castle stands proudly on a hill.
3. Visitors can see it clearly.
4. Patiently visitors wait at the castle gate.

Forming Adverbs (pages 164–165)
   Change each word into an adverb. Write the
new word.

1. safe	3. watchful	5. fresh	7. proud
2. dangerous	4. clever	6. new	8. strange

Writing: A Description (pages 172–174)

Think about a store you know. Plan, write, and
edit a description of it. Use a lot of details. Tell
what you can see, hear, touch, smell, and taste.
Use space-order words. Then edit your description.
Copy it in your best handwriting. If you need
more help, read pages 172–174 again.

Pronouns (pages 186–187, 188–189)

Number your paper from *1* to *7*. Read each
sentence. Write the correct pronoun.

1. Nancy and (I/me) read a story.
2. (She/Her) likes to read about people.
3. She and (I/me) liked the book.
4. (They/It) was about a man named Daniel Parkway.
5. (Him/He) carried mail in the 1600s.
6. (Him/He) had to travel on very poor roads.
7. People gave (him/he) their mail to deliver.

Using *I* or *Me* (pages 190–191)

Number your paper from *1* to *8*. Decide which
pronoun should complete each sentence. Write the
pronoun.

1. Vicky and (I/me) are good friends.
2. (I/Me) told her about my dream.
3. She listened to (I/me) carefully.

4. (I/Me) dreamed we were in a movie.

5. (I/Me) dreamed something chased us.

6. It was after Vicky and (I/me).

7. She and (I/me) ran.

8. Then (I/me) woke up.

Pronouns in Sentences (pages 192–193)

Find the pronoun in each sentence. Write it.
Label it *Subject* or *Not Subject.*

1. We snorkle around the reef.

2. The reef seems very strange to us.

3. It is so long.

4. Many creatures and plants live around it.

5. They are very unusual.

6. Dick and Paula swim close to them.

7. He counts all the fish.

8. Then I dive down to the bottom of the reef.

9. Carol follows me.

Contractions with Pronouns (pages 202–203)

Change each underlined pronoun and verb into a
contraction. Write the sentences using the
contractions.

1. I have counted many fish.

2. She is my friend.

3. You would like the reef.

4. It is very beautiful there.

5. I am going back again.

6. We will dive together.

7. They are coming with us.

8. You are going to like it.

Too Many Nouns (pages 204–205)

Read each pair of sentences. Find the repeated words. Rewrite the second sentence. Use a pronoun where needed.

1. The book was very old. The book told about a sea trip.
2. We read about a leather ship. The ship was not big.
3. Tim and his friends built the boat. Tim and his friends called it *Brendan.*
4. The sailors had many adventures during the trip. Many dangerous things happened to the sailors.
5. Tim sailed from Iceland to Canada. Tim was a hero.

Too Many Pronouns (pages 206–207)

Read each sentence. Find the subject nouns and pronouns that mean the same thing. Rewrite the sentence so that it has just one subject.

1. The Mountain gorillas they are very rare.
2. These animals they are also very shy.
3. The gorillas they live in groups of families.
4. Each group it can be large or small.
5. One gorilla he is the leader of each group.

Writing: An Argument (pages 214–216)

Plan, write, and edit an argument that will persuade a reader. Write the opinion first. Then write two good reasons for your opinion. Write the ending.

Matching Subjects and Verbs (pages 228–229, 230–231)
Write the correct verb for each subject.

1. Cindy, Lou, and Mike (sell/sells) flowers and food.
2. They (work/works) long hours.
3. Cindy (weed/weeds) the garden.
4. Every evening Lou (water/waters) the garden.
5. Mike (pick/picks) the ripe vegetables.
6. He (cut/cuts) fresh flowers, too.
7. Then the children (take/takes) them to their stand.

Using *Has* and *Have* (page 232)
Complete each sentence with *has* or *have*.

1. We (has/have) many pen pals.
2. Kevin (has/have) pen pals in many countries.
3. Nedda (has/have) lots of pen pals, too.
4. She (has/have) stacks of letters from them.
5. The letters (has/have) colorful stamps.
6. I (has/have) only three pen pals.
7. Our pen pals (has/have) our pictures.

Helping Verbs (page 233)
Write these sentences. Underline the main verbs.
Circle the helping verbs.

1. I am having a beach party.
2. You are coming to it.
3. First we will catch lots of fish.

4. Jim and Reiko are holding the net in the water.
5. I am planning a dinner.
6. Rachel is making poi from taro roots.
7. A boy was washing the taro roots.

Punctuating Conversations (pages 240–241)
Each sentence has one mistake. Write the sentence correctly. Underline the speaker tag.

1. Dan asked "Why isn't your nose twelve inches long?"
2. "Because it's not a foot, Jan said.
3. "What do you call a potato that yells?" asked Jan
4. A fresh vegetable," Dan answered.
5. "What did the big rose say to the baby rose, Dan asked.
6. Jan replied, "hi, bud!"

Irregular Verbs (pages 234–235, 246–247, 248–249)
Write the correct verb to complete each sentence.

1. They had (come/came) to the cliff in a rowboat.
2. They had (come/came) to have a picnic.
3. They (did/done) this every summer.
4. The waves (took/taken) the rowboat out to sea.
5. They have (sit/sat) on the cliff all morning.
6. Silently the children (ate/eaten) their lunch.
7. They had (ate/eaten) all the food.
8. Then they (see/saw) a boat and began to shout.
9. They shouted, "Help has (come/came)!"

Contractions With *Not* (pages 250–251)
  Write the contractions of these words.

1. are not   **3.** do not   **5.** have not   **7.** was not
2. cannot   **4.** does not   **6.** is not   **8.** will not

Avoiding Double Negatives (pages 252–253)
  Write each negative word or contraction.

1. Scientists have never seen a black hole in space.
2. No one has ever seen a black hole there.
3. There isn't a picture of a black hole in the library.
4. There are none in the newspapers.

  Choose the correct word for each sentence.

1. Wes can't go (nowhere/anywhere) tomorrow.
2. The moon doesn't have (no/any) light of its own.
3. Don't do (nothing/anything) for a few hours.
4. He (can/can't) never talk slowly.

Writing: A Story (pages 260–262)
  Plan, write, and edit a story about something
you choose. (Example: A wild animal has escaped
from the zoo.) Introduce the characters (animals
and people). Give the setting. Tell what the
problem is. Explain how the problem is solved.
Don't forget the title! Edit your story. Copy it in
your best handwriting. If you need help, read
pages 260–262.

Index

light italic print *(123)* = Review the Basics, Unit Test, Keep Practicing, More Practice
dark italic print *(123)* = Handbook

WH-questions, 34–35, *37, 47,* 80–81, 82–83, 84-86, 87, *92,* 122, 125–126, 136, 290–291, ***317, 332***

Words

that persuade, 200–201, *269*

with almost the same meaning. *See* Synonyms.

with different meanings. *See* Antonyms.

with *-er* and *-est. See* Adjectives, that compare.

with prefixes. *See* Prefixes.

Writing

general guidelines, ***327–328***

models, 38–39, 82–83, 122–123, 212–213, 302–303

See also Argument; Business Letter; Description; Invitation; Paragraph; Report; Story.

Yes-No questions, 32–33, *37, 47, 92,* ***317, 332***